BECOMING YOUR OWN BANKER

THE INFINITE BANKING CONCEPT

By

R. Nelson Nash

Infinite Banking Concepts - Birmingham, Alabama

© Copyright 2000 R. Nelson Nash

Fifth Edition, 2008, Third Printing

Infinite Banking Concepts

2957 Old Rocky Ridge Road

Birmingham, AL 35243

Email: david.stearns@charter.net

www.infinitebanking.org

205-276-2977

ISBN-0-9726316-1-5

ISBN-13 978-0-9726316-1-7

Cover Design by Nathan Ingram, Brilliant New Media LLC

INTRODUCTION TO THE FIFTH EDITION

Becoming Your Own Banker - The Infinite Banking Concept is a text for a ten-hour course of instruction about the power of dividend-paying whole life insurance. It is not a sales tool for life insurance agents. It is education that the life insurance industry should have taught during the last 200 years. Unfortunately, the industry has concentrated on the death benefit qualities of the contract and has neglected to adequately describe the financing capabilities that it presents for the policy owners. Ironically, life insurance companies must put premium income to work in various investments in order to pay the death claims.

This book demonstrates that your need for finance, during your lifetime, is much greater than your need for protection. Solve for this need though this instrument and you will end up with more life insurance than the companies will issue on you. Most everyone is familiar with the fact that one can borrow from a whole life policy, but because of how little premiums they pay, there is limited access to money to finance major items needed during a lifetime. Yet, the need for financing for the typical person is extensive. Really, all this book adds to the equation is scale.

The fact that the principles have been there all along and no one taught them to me makes me rather angry! Had I known them, life would have been much simpler and much more profitable. Someone should have recognized them and taught them long ago, but this didn't take place because of the mindset that predominates in the entire financial world.

It is written for the layman, not for financial advisors, but all life agents should be thoroughly knowledgeable of its content and practice. Again, unfortunately, this is not the case. Very few of them have more than a rudimentary understanding of its qualities.

The whole idea is to recapture the interest that one is paying to banks and finance companies for the major items that we need during a lifetime, such as automobiles, major appliances, education, homes, investment opportunities, business equipment, etc.

This book is not about investments of any kind. It is about how one *finances* the things of life, which can certainly include investments. It is not about rates of return. As time goes by interest rates are up and interest rates are down — but the process of banking goes on no matter what is happening. It is a well known fact that banks make more money during times of low interest rates than when rates are high.

A word of caution is in order — later in the book you will be looking at illustrations of life insurance policies that show how the concept works as compared with how most folks go about solving their financial affairs. Most of the illustrations were developed in 2000 and represent dividend scales in effect at that time. Presently, interest earnings are lower and, hence, dividend scales are lower. But in comparison with other methods of financing the things of life, the difference in results remains the same.

It is not a procedure to "get rich quickly." To the contrary, it requires long range planning. I'm educated as a forester, having worked in that field as a consultant for ten years; I tend to think seventy years in the future. I won't be here — and neither will you — but there is no reason not to behave in this manner. "Plan as if you are going to live forever and live as if you are going to die today" appears to me to be a good thought. One can learn how to plan and act intergenerationally. That's one of the primary advantages of having been a forester. I learned to think beyond the lifespan of my current generation.

Becoming Your Own Banker is not a tax-qualified idea of any sort. The Income Tax Law, as we know it today, has only been around since 1913. Life insurance has been around for over 200 years and is not a creature of any tax code. It is nothing more than like-minded people contracting with one another to solve a financial problem.

There is no such thing as "having too much money in the bank." Wealth must reside somewhere. What better place to have it reside than here?

From this residence one can do anything that

one can conceive. This is an advantage that most folks ignore in their thought process, and therefore, limits their effectiveness.

Let me make it abundantly clear—I am not talking about a *bank* in the conventional sense of the word. I am demonstrating that one can use dividend-paying whole life insurance to solve one's need for finance throughout one's life.

Hopefully, this book will give you a new perspective on the idea of "retirement." I prefer to use the words, "passive income." That is money coming in that you can count on and you don't do anything to earn it at that time. Study the illustrations carefully and you will see that very high premium, dividend-paying, whole life insurance is the ultimate vehicle to produce such income.

The Infinite Banking Concept is a major paradigm shift for most folks. It will require several thorough readings for a full understanding of its message. The concept is not complicated, it is just different from the way the majority thinks and behaves. In fact, it is the ultimate in simplicity.

There is an extensive reading list in the book and you are encouraged to read them all. Education is an on-going process and there is no such thing as having "arrived" in knowledge.

There have been many people that have had a glimpse of what this book is all about but none, to my knowledge; no one has put together a comprehensive rationale such as you will see here. Read it with an open mind and you will discover a whole new financial world.

"The problem in America isn't so much what people don't know; the problem is what people think they know that just ain't so."
- Will Rogers

DEDICATION

"To Mary, my joy and inspiration."

ACKNOWLEDGMENTS

To my children-Debby and Jake, Barry and Janel, Kim and Dave - for their belief in me and for being such good practitioners of the banking concept. The same thing goes for the inspiration of Patricia K. Walker.

To Frank Vawter, who in the beginning, raised some key thoughts and questions that led me to look deeper into just what is happening in a dividend-paying life insurance policy with a mutual company. Kent Basson, "Buddy" Mann, Roland Nelson, Fred Moss, Billy King, Keith Burton, Vince D'Addona and Rob Colburn were also instrumental in this respect.

A special thanks to Paul Cleveland, Jim Thorington, and Jacqui Neuwirth for their expert assistance in proofreading the manuscript.

And to Mike Mallory for putting this book all together and getting it printed.

Thanks to you all for your contribution. I am very grateful for your friendship and your help.

CONTENTS

PART I - BECOMING YOUR OWN BANKER

Someone made the comment that "If some authoritative power distributed all the money in the world equally among all the people in the world, within ten years time 97% of all the money would be under the control of 3% of the people." I suppose that there is no way ever to measure the validity of such a statement, but I have the feeling that most people would agree that it is probably close to the truth. Even if the proportions were somewhat moderated—say 75% of the money would be under the control of 25% of the people—why do you think that this phenomenon happens?

Perhaps some of the answer lies in the fact that most folks know next to nothing about the process of banking and its importance to their lives and their well being. Banking is *the* most important business in the world! Without it, all business comes to a screeching halt. Whenever a business transaction takes place, money must flow from one party to another in a relatively short time or, otherwise, nothing takes place. That flow of money must come from a supply source, a reservoir. That is the essence of what the banking business is all about; someo*ne* or some *organization* has control of a pool of money that can (and must) flow, at a cost, to meet some need.

There is only one pool of money in the world. The fact that this pool is managed by any number of institutions: banks, insurance companies, corporations, and individuals in various countries with various currency denominations is incidental. To argue otherwise would be the equivalent of someone looking at the globe and observing that the Amazon River in South America flows into the Atlantic Ocean and commenting that "this has nothing to do with the Indian Ocean on the other side of the globe."

Nonsense! It is all part of a system. Observe that about 75% of the Earth's surface is covered by water. The sun heats it up and some of it evaporates into the atmosphere causing wind currents. The currents take the water vapor around the earth and it precipitates out in the form of rain, sleet and snow—and somewhere along the way some of it *flows through you and me.* Without it we die! That makes it of vital importance. Pray tell, where does it end up? Right! Back in the oceans!

The banking business is somewhat like that. Money flows from the pool through our hands to meet our needs—but somewhere in the process it all ends up back into the banking system. It is all a matter of "how much of the banking function do you control as it relates to your needs." This book is all about how to create your own banking system so that *you* can control 100% of *your needs. Becoming your own banker*! Give it your close attention and it can make a radical improvement in your financial future.

For I know the plans I have for you" declares *the LORD. "plans to prosper you and not to harm you, plans to give you hope and a future.*
- Jeremiah 29:11

HOW THE INFINITE BANKING CONCEPT GOT STARTED

First, a bit about my background. I was educated as a forester, graduating from the University of Georgia in 1952. A large portion of the root thought of this concept is coming from the study of forest finance—the fact that you are dealing with compound interest over a long period of time with no taxation on the build-up. The reverse fact is that you must make an investment and *you won't see any result* for *that same long period!* In the forestry world you must think many years into the future. I worked as a forestry consultant for about 10 years.

Some of it is coming from the life insurance business. I made a good living in life insurance sales for over 30 years. Knowing how dividend-paying life insurance works is an essential ingredient to it all. Most people have a minimal understanding of the subject, *including* the home office personnel at life insurance companies! That is strange, but very true.

Lastly, it was strongly influenced by my experience in the real estate business. Timber is a form of real estate as well as the land on which it grows, so I have been around real estate for all my working life and I developed a strong interest in the subject, studying many books on it. If you read these books, the central message is not about real estate at all—it is about the magic of *leverage!* Essentially, they all say, "Buy some real estate, borrow the money to pay for it, (because you are *always* dealing with borrowed money—you either borrow money and pay interest, or you use your own money and give up interest that you could have earned) pay interest for a while, then sell the property. All you have given up is the interest you have paid out. That leverage is *wonderful!"*

That is all true—as long as things are going the way the "financial geniuses" describe it. But they *never* tell you what happens when the *lever goes the other way!* Frankly, I made some money in the late '70s doing it the way the "geniuses" explained it (someone remarked that "financial genius is a *rising market")*. There were several successful ventures in a row and it looked like there was no end to this bonanza. I could do no wrong! The ventures got bigger and bigger and I got more and more involved, buying a large number of acres of rural property. And then I got into real estate development. With the profits from one small parcel, my wife and I went to Europe in 1977 and spent a month! Would you believe it—I have *never* seen that property yet? And I did it all according to "the book by the financial geniuses"—leverage—other people's money. Just have your Realtor find such a deal and attend to all the particulars for you—and then sell it for you! Marvelous!

There was no logical reason not to *expand.* And so I did. The interest rate (prime) at that time was 8%, but you must pay 1.5% over "prime" (now referred to as *base rate*), because the Bankers are *not* lending you money because you have real estate—they are doing it because *they think you can make payments!* Why else would they require personal endorsement on the loan? And you must renew the notes every 90 days—at the current interest rate. I got accustomed to paying 9.5% and that was just normal. And then, along came 1981 and 1982. The prime rate rose and "peaked" at 21.5%!! Add 1.5% on top of that and you see my situation—23% interest on $500,000!! That amounts to $67,500 of interest per year *that I was not expecting to pay!*

When this happens to you, what do you do? Go ask the "financial geniuses" who recommended that you do this, "What do I do, now?" If you can find them, they may mumble something about "selling the real estate." But, where do you find a *fool* that will buy it under those circumstances! Of course, everything will sell if you get the price low enough, but losing five times what you paid for it is hardly a good way out.

But, so far, you have heard only a part of my story. The beginning of my "awakening" was in November 1980 when our first grandchild was born. Interest rates had begun to zoom upward. That was Bunker Hunt's heyday—you remember him? Bunker and his brother were going to "corner" the silver market—and as a result silver prices increased higher than anything, relatively speaking. Gold went up to $800 per oz. And so, "drug junkies" started supporting their drug habit by stealing silver from homes. While my wife was visiting our new granddaughter some 60 miles away for several days, the thieves broke into our home at 3:00 p.m. and "cleaned us out." Have you ever been burglarized? You won't believe what they can do to a house in just a few minutes. Luckily, I got to clean up the mess. If my wife had seen it I don't believe she would ever feel comfortable in that house again.

Two months later my 52 year-old brother dropped dead from a heart attack while playing racquetball with a son. Poor selection of ancestors—our father died at age 64 from the same problem.

Five months later our second granddaughter was born out in Hawaii. Five weeks later her parents discovered that *the baby had cancer!* I didn't even know that babies could get cancer. She went on chemotherapy when she was six weeks old. Six months later she went through surgery to remove the tumor on her right adrenal gland. The cancer was a *neuroblastoma*, a very rare kind that attacks children. The lesions had involved her liver and she had to go back on chemotherapy for several more treatments. My story has a good part—she is now 25 years old and is cured!! We have seen a *miracle!*

And now for the bad financial news—it was that summer that interest rates went to 23 percent—and there I stood owing $500,000 under those circumstances. When a number of bad things like this occur in fairly rapid succession it can increase the quality of your prayer life dramatically! The basic idea revealed in the Infinite Banking Concept was born over a period of many, many months at 3:00 to 4:00 a.m. in the *kneeling position* praying, "Lord, please, show me a way out of this financial nightmare that I have created for myself." The answer came back about like a baseball bat across the eyes. "You are standing in the midst of everything it takes to get out—but you don't see it because you look at things like everyone else. You can get to money, during these awful times, at 5% to 8% from three different life insurance companies through policies *that you own.* The only thing that limits how much you can get to is the same thing they tell you at the bank when you ask them how big of a check you can write—*how much have you put in?"*

If I had not been accustomed to paying very large premiums it is doubtful that I would have seen the message. Hardship often helps us to see things to which we are normally blind. It was evident to me that I needed to increase my life insurance premiums dramatically to create a pool of cash values from which to borrow to pay off the bankers that I owed. But, I owed $500,000! How could I do both? Honest introspection revealed that I *could revise my spending pattern.* This was a starting place. When I started teaching others to design their financial dealings along these lines my income tripled. Practically everyone thought I was crazy—it was opposite to what all the "experts" said. But an objective look at the facts of how life insurance worked, plus reason and logic—and continued sessions of intense prayer for guidance has proved that the system works!!

Maybe you have found yourself in such a financial prison—or maybe you want to develop a system that will keep you *out!* Maybe yours is smaller or greater. Whatever, the principles are the same and they will serve you well. It requires understanding—and it requires discipline to implement the idea, but it can change your life dramatically—even beyond your fondest dreams!

My people are destroyed from lack of knowledge. Because you have rejected knowledge, I also reject you as my priests; because you have ignored the law of your God, I also will ignore your children.

- Hosea 4:6

IMAGINATION

"Imagination is more important than knowledge"
—Albert Einstein

The Infinite Banking Concept is an exercise in imagination, reason, logic and prophecy. So to start out, let's begin with the part about imagination.

To help stimulate your imagination let's go back in time to the late 1700's—the German Schoolmaster was having trouble with his boys that day—they were rowdy 7-year olds. He wanted to quiet them down—and to punish them, so he gave them a problem. "Add up all the numbers—one through one hundred."

The boys got their slates down and started to work on the problem. His plan seemed to be working, except for one boy who just sat there staring out the window. Presently he picked up his slate, wrote down a number and turned it in to the Schoolmaster. Since *his* was the only correct answer, the Schoolmaster took note of the fact and asked the boy how he did it.

The boy said, "I visualized a line with the figure '1' on the left side and the figure '100' on the right side. Then I cut the line at the halfway point, 50, and folded the scale to the left so that there were now two lines that were parallel. 100 was lined up with 1 on the left side and 50 and 51 were lined up on the right side. Adding the two numbers on each end of the scales was easy to do. I noticed that *all the pairs of numbers in between* on the scale added up to 101, too, and that there were 50 pairs of the sets of 101. Multiplying 101 times 50 is simple! The total was 5,050."

Thereafter the young boy received special tutoring and he later became one of the three greatest mathematicians of all time—his name was Karl Gauss!

Young Gauss did not *invent* that fact—he *discovered* what God had done already! He discovered a relationship between numbers that is *fixed* and *nothing can be done to change it*.

Now that we understand this fact we can take a shortcut in getting the answer. Whenever we are adding anything beginning with one and ending with a multiple such as ten, one hundred, one thousand, etc. you simply pick the mid-point (in the first case cited above, 50) and simply put that same figure alongside it. (5050). So to add all the numbers 1 through 1,000, you simply pick the mid-point, 500 and put 500 alongside it (500,500). Simple! And *accurate*! It is *fixed*. Try to pass some law to change that fact and you are engaging in an exercise in futility.

Nevertheless, somewhere in the past I have heard that a legislature in some State tried to get the mathematical term, "Pi," *changed from* 3.1416 to 3.00 because it was too *complicated and cumbersome*! These demi-gods could not conceive that they were dealing with a *fixed relationship* that *they could not change* and had no authority over. But therein lies the story of mankind since time began!

THE GROCERY STORE

To continue with the imagination exercise, I would like you to examine the process of getting into a business in which you are both a *consumer* and a *seller* of the same thing. (There is a very significant reason for this exercise, so bear with me). A grocery store will easily meet these qualifications—everyone consumes groceries, and someone has to perform the distribution function. You have an unlimited market. Everyone is a potential customer—as well as you and your family and maybe some other "captive customers."

You start it all by studying what the grocery business is all about, all the things that are necessary to be successful as an entrepreneur in this field. This is going to take some time and expense. When you feel competent to start the venture you must now find a good location for the business. The real estate folks say there are three important things about real estate—location, location, and location. For such a property you are going to pay dearly. This is not an overnight activity, either. You are going to have to spend some time locating the right place.

Then you must construct a very nice looking building on the property. It must have a well-arranged interior with attractive equipment and fixtures and display cases. All this is necessary because your competition has been hard at work for years in attracting customers. Customers are going to do business with stores that are convenient, that look good, that have quality merchandise—and low prices! This means that the building, etc., is going to cost you a lot of money.

Now you must stock the store with groceries. The merchandise must be of good quality, attractively displayed, and have competitive prices. Your employees must be attentive to customer needs, courteous, and neat. This is going to cost you a lot of money, too. You open the front door for customers—they come in and load their carts with groceries and take them by the cashier who collects their money at the front of the store. This is going to leave empty spaces in the display of goods. Your "hired help" is busy cruising the aisles, noticing where goods have been sold and quickly going to the storeroom at the back of the store to get more things to fill up those spaces. It is imperative that the store appears "fully stocked" at any given time. The customers demand it. Have you ever been to a grocery store that was only "partially stocked?" Did you continue to patronize that store—or did you take your business to another store that was more conscious of this quality?

All this means that you are going to have to re-stock the storeroom at other intervals to ensure that you have immediate access to a bountiful supply of goods. The objective of the business is to provide you with income and to build a business that you will eventually sell to someone else to provide you with retirement income.

Once you get this all set up and in operation, the difference between the "back door" and the "front door" is a very good living—*if* you can *turn* the inventory enough times per year. If you sell a can of peas for 60 cents at the front door, you have to replace it at the back door at a cost of 57 cents. (I have found this to be a shocking revelation to most everyone). Grocery stores operate on a very small margin on such items. The can of peas sitting on the shelf for sale represents inventory. You must turn the inventory 15 times just to break even! There is all that interest you must pay on the huge sums of money you have borrowed to buy the land, the building, the signs, advertising, payroll and fringe benefits, utilities, legal fees, accounting, etc., to name a few. Turn it 17 times and you will be profitable. If you can turn the inventory 20 times per year you can retire early! Something dramatic happens once you get over the hump.

It all reminds me of a phenomenon in physics—take a pail of water to the seaside (I want you at sea level) and heat it to 210 degrees Fahrenheit and all you have is very hot water. But if you heat it up to 212 degrees Fahrenheit you have live steam with unbelievable power. The steam engine changed the world! But it doesn't happen until you get past 212 degrees. Lots of heat goes into the process up to the boiling point but the dramatic power comes suddenly.

Thus far, the business looks pretty simple. But now, we complicate the picture. Assuming that you are a male, married, with children, where is your wife going to shop for groceries—your store, or somewhere else? Further assuming that she chooses correctly—your store—she comes into the front door and fills her cart with groceries. Here comes the complicated part. Please pay close attention! This point is critical and requires scrupulous honesty. Out of which door is she likely to take the groceries, front or back?

When delivering lectures, I ask this question and wait for answers. An amazing number will readily admit that, "In all probability, she wants to go out the back door, avoiding the cashier at the front door." This is a very polite description of theft! Probably more businesses have been destroyed or severely limited by this sort of behavior than anything else. It is a feeling among owners and those related to them that, "This is our business and we can do anything we want to!" Unless this misunderstanding is curbed, the business is doomed. Consider this—over an extended period of time, can she go out the back door with her groceries without the "hired help" witnessing her act? I think not. So, what will the "hired help" do as a result? They are going to steal groceries, too. You can predict it with certainty.

If you are unaware of the prevalence of theft in the retail business, do yourself a favor and make friends with someone who owns or manages a retail business. Then ask about how common is theft by employees. The answer will probably shock you. Question—who pays for all this theft? The customers who go past the cashier with their goods and pay for them, that's who! It can't come from anywhere else. Theft is devastating. Just consider, if your wife steals one can of peas, you have to sell 20 to make up for it.

There is another thing that makes owners and their family members want to go out the back door. Every business in the United States has a "silent partner"—the Internal Revenue Service. If your wife goes out the front door and pays retail for her groceries just like everyone else, then your store makes more money than if she went out the back door. And the IRS posture is "the more you make—the more we take."

But, suppose we could have a situation where the profits from the sale of groceries are not subject to income taxes. Now, we have eliminated one of the incentives to go out the back door with goods. The only problem that remains is the human instinct to want to use the back door privilege. This urge must be overcome. Your business is at stake.

However, you and your family (plus maybe some others) are captive customers for your store. You all are not going somewhere else to buy groceries. By now, you should realize that if you charge these captive customers wholesale prices, you have defeated the purpose of the business—to provide income for you and to build a business that you will eventually sell and use the proceeds for retirement income. If you charge them retail prices, you are going in the right direction. But, these are *captive* customers! Why not charge these folks 62 cents for the can of peas? The extra two cents will go directly to additional capital to *buy more cans of peas to sell to the other customers!* Hopefully, you can see what continued use of this practice can do to the profitability of your business. Do this over a long number of years and your record books will show a superior profitability picture.

When you sell your business some years later, you are in competition with someone else who has not obeyed these principles. He and his family members took their groceries out the back door, etc. The record books of this man's business will never look as good as yours. That is, *if* he is still in business! In all probability he has gone out of business long ago. But, even if he is still around, can you guess which business will bring the better price? Yours! And this makes it possible for you to "clip larger coupons" at retirement time. I hope that you have learned this little lesson well. We will re-visit the grocery store later on in the book. If you understand the grocery store, the rest of learning how to be your own banker is "a piece of cake!"

THE PROBLEM

When Jesus saw him lying there and learned that he had been in this condition for a long time, he asked him, "Do you want to get well?" — John 5:6

Several years ago I did a good bit of study on the spending habits of American families. Since that time I have kept an eye on the figures and the proportion of income allocated to each category. This seems to be the current situation, which doesn't seem to change all that much. I build scenarios around the "All-American family" because I don't want people to think you have to be rich to create a banking system that can handle all your needs for finance. This young man is 29 years old and is making $28,500 per year after taxes. What does he do with the after-tax income?

Twenty percent is spent on transportation, thirty percent is spent on housing, forty-five percent is spent on "living" (clothes, groceries, contributions to religious and charitable causes, boat payments, casualty insurance on cars, vacations, etc. Many of these items are financed by charge cards or bank notes. The balance is *financed* by paying cash for them—and thus, giving up interest that could be earned, otherwise). He is saving less than five percent of disposable income. But, to be as generous as possible, let's assume that he is saving *ten percent* and spending only forty percent on living expenses. This is giving him every

benefit of the doubt on the matter of savings. Just remember, the real situation is at least twice as bad as what will be depicted!

The problem is that all these items are *financed* by other banking organizations. An automobile financing package for this hypothetical person is $10,550 for 48 months with an interest rate of at least 8.5% with payments of $260.05 per month. But, if you will check with the sales manager of an automobile agency you will find that 95% of the cars that are traded in *are not paid for!* This means, at the end of 30 months, if the car is traded, 21% of every payment dollar is *interest.* Even if he goes the full four years, the portion of every payment made is still 20%! This means that the interest portion of every dollar spent is perpetual. It never seems to dawn that the *volume of interest* is the real issue, not the *annual percentage rate.* For a real thrill, go to see the sales manager of the high priced cars and ask him what percentage of the cars that leave their car lot are *leased.* The answer will probably be 75%, or more! This is worse than financing a car purchase.

When you go to the Doctor's office to get a shot of some kind, the criteria is not the *rate* at which the medicine is injected into you—it is the *volume!* Too little, and it won't do any good—too much and it can kill you!

Now, let's move to the housing situation. This young man can qualify for a 30 year fixed-rate mortgage in the amount of about $93,000 at a fixed interest rate of 7% APR with payments of $618.75 and closing costs of some $2,500. The problem is

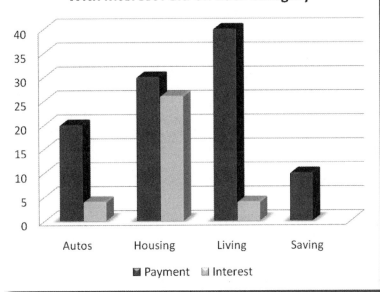

Annual Pattern of Spending Compared With Interest Paid on Each Category

Categories: Autos, Housing, Living, Saving
Legend: ■ Payment ▨ Interest

that within 5 years he will move to another city, across town, or refinance the mortgage. Something happens to a mortgage within 5 years. Including the closing costs and interest paid out during these 60 months he had paid $39,625, but only $5,458 has gone to reduce the loan. This means that $34,167 has gone to interest and closing costs. Divide the amount paid out into the interest and closing costs and you find that *86% of every dollar paid out goes to the cost of financing!* If he sells the house in less than 5 years, it is worse. This proportion never gets any better because he takes on a new mortgage and starts all over again. He thinks that he is "buying" a house, but all he is really doing is making the wheels of the banking business and the real estate business –in that order—turn.

In the next segment of his spending pattern—the living expenses—you will find that the interest on his boat payments, credit card interest, plus the cost of casualty insurance on the automobiles, etc. will rival in volume the interest he is paying on the two automobiles. (Later on in this book you will learn how to self-insure for comprehensive and collision insurance on automobiles).

Now, add up all the interest he is paying out and you find that 34.5 cents of every disposable dollar paid out is *interest.* For the average All-American male this proportion *never changes.* Let's assume that he is trying to save 10% of his disposable income, *which is twice the average savings rate in America.* That means that we have a 3.45 to 1 ratio of interest paid out as compared to savings. If you will get this young man together with his peers at a coffee break or some such gathering and have one of them suggest that they discuss financial matters, I can predict what they will talk about—getting a *high rate of return* on the portion they are saving! Meanwhile, every participant in the conversation is doing the above! What a tragedy! But that is how they have learned to conduct their financial affairs.

All of this reminds me of a phenomenon in the airplane world. I have been flying, as a pilot, since 1947, and I learned early on that you could not fly an airplane through a vacuum. It must go through an *environment*! We have all seen the weather maps with the "HIGHs" and the "LOWs." In the Northern Hemisphere the HIGHs turn clockwise. A large one can cover 75% or more of the U. S. So picture this situation: You are in Birmingham, AL with an airplane that can fly 100 miles per hour and your destination is Chicago. The only problem is that you have a *headwind* of 345 miles per hour! Regardless of what your airspeed indicator says, your airplane is moving toward Miami at 245 miles per hour! If you want to go to Chicago, that's a very good time to get your airplane on the ground—quickly!

Have some patience and the air mass will move on—they *always* do. When the HIGH gets directly over the top of you there is no headwind. You are now covering the ground at 100 m.p.h.. And now, the "arrival syndrome" comes into play. You conclude that "you just can't do any better than this. This is the ultimate situation." Nonsense! Have more patience and the air mass will continue to move on. Now you have a *tailwind of 345 m.p.h.!* Plus your airplane is moving at a speed of 100 m.p.h.. Your *ground speed* is 445 m.p.h.! That is *impressive,* isn't it? But, you see, it is much more impressive than most people think. *Everything you do in the financial world is compared with what everyone else is doing!* Ninety-five percent of the American public is doing the equivalent of flying with a 345 m.p.h. headwind. If you have a 345 m.p.h. tailwind, the difference between you and them is *twice the wind!* That is a difference of 690 m.p.h.!

Most people in this situation concentrate all their attention to trying to make the airplane go 105 m.p.h.! They would do well to spend their energy instead on controlling the environment in which they fly. You can't do that in the airplane world—but *you can* in the financial world. You can do it by controlling the "banking equation" as it relates to you. That's what this book is about—creating a perpetual "tailwind" to everything you do in the financial world. (There are many "financial gurus" out there who are praising the matter of "getting out of debt" but they never address this fact). This is the unique message of *The Infinite Banking Concept.*

Somehow or another, it never dawns on most financial gurus that you *can* control the financial environment in which you operate. Perhaps it is caused by lack of imagination, but whatever the cause, learning to control it is *the most profitable* thing that you can do over a lifetime.

CREATING A BANK LIKE THE ONES YOU ALREADY KNOW ABOUT

If you are going to create a bank like the ones you already know about, there are a number of steps you must go through. Like the grocery business we discussed earlier, you must first study the business so that you have a firm grip on what it is all about and feel that you can run such a business. Without this confidence you are fighting a lost cause. It's a jungle out there!

Next, you must get some Capital—*money*—and it had better be in the order of $20 million or more. This money must sit in some other bank in a very liquid form, that is, it is earning a very low interest rate.

Then you go to the Banking Commissioner's office and apply for a Bank Charter. Bear in mind that the Commissioner doesn't hand out charters indiscriminately. The chance of your getting one at this point is probably less than 100 to 1. There are a lot of other folks that would like to be bankers. You must wait your turn. Whenever I hear the word, Commissioner, I always think of an iceberg—only 10% appears above the water! There is a lot going on that is unseen. At this point you need to use your imagination. The bottom line is that you are going to spend a lot of time and money in this phase of creating your bank. Years are likely to have passed before you finally win the coveted charter. In the meantime, you have probably gone through the part about a good location and suitable building. This, too, is all at considerable expense.

Now you are finally in business as a bank. You must make your bank known by lots of advertising and inducing people to make deposits to your bank. Why do you think they would deposit their money with your bank when they could easily do business with established banks that have been there for years? Right! You are going to have to pay them something better than they are getting at their current banking connection. Do you notice, thus far, that you have been paying out money for years in getting this business established?

In his book, *PAPER MONEY*, author Adam Smith has this to say: "A banker cannot make a loan unless he has a deposit. It seems a little silly to state that so baldly, but if three college-educated Americans in ten don't know that we have to import oil, I don't feel so bad about saying something bald. Banks do not lend their money. They lend the money somebody else has left there." Later on in the book he goes on to explain: "When you start up a bank, you have to put in some capital. Then you get some deposits, and then you lend the deposits. In a proper bank these three items bear a prudent relation to one another. If you are a little country bank with a capital of $100,000, it would be very imprudent of you to loan Brazil $50 million. So you want a prudent relationship between the capital and the assets, which is to say the loans on the books, and between the loans and the deposits. In the Western countries the financial agents of the government are there with a definition of prudence."

Yes, there are financial agents of the government with a definition of prudence, but they still did not preclude massive bank failures in the mid-1980's in America. During this same time the Asian banking community "could do no wrong." They were hailed as financial geniuses. Now there are bank failures in Asia that are much greater than those that occurred in the U. S. My point is that we are not dealing here with *man-made laws*—they have failed miserably. We are dealing with relations among people, i.e. God-made laws. You disobey them at your peril.

A case comes to mind. In September 1983 the First National Bank of Midland, Texas (the richest city in America per capita at that time) had a loan portfolio of $1.5 billion. And 26% of those loans were *non-performing*, i.e. they were not getting the money back.

This is a big "downer" in the banking business. When this sort of thing happens someone has to support the situation, which is normally the function of the stockholders. Because of losses the stockholders' equity lost 87% of its value down to $12 million. Remember the prudent relationships that Adam Smith outlined above. $12 million in capital in relation to $1.5 Billion in loans is a shaky bank!

When the public found out about it, can you predict what happened to bank deposits at First National at this time? Right! They decreased by $500 million. Remember, this is what banks lend—deposits made by their customers. This accelerated their decline.

This all sounds pretty ominous, but you haven't seen anything yet. You must add the "multiplier effect" of bank lending practices. Practically no one is aware that, when you make a deposit of $1,000 at your favorite bank, they can now lend out $10,000 as a result of your deposit. It is called the "fractional reserve lending system," that is, they are creating money out of thin air. (My own description of what they are doing is *the world's largest con game*). It is all predicated on the theory that "everyone is not going to withdraw their money at the same time." For a complete treatise on what is going on in banking I suggest, no, I *beg you* to read *The Case Against The Fed,* by Murray Rothbard. You can get it at the Ludwig von Mises Institute located in Auburn, AL.

The First National Bank hired a new CEO to come in and "put out the fire," but it was too late. Two months later they were out of business. A more complete picture of what happened to this bank appeared in the December issue of a drilling magazine. Reading "between the lines" it was pretty evident that a lot of those non-performing loans were made to the members of the board of directors. They were making loans to themselves to invest in the oil business where they were going to "make a killing" and neglecting to repay the loans. There was a big energy crisis just a while before this. When the oil business returned to normal these folks lost both their oil business *and* their banking business. Had they repaid their loans plus interest, their bank would have still been in operation but greed prevailed and "did them in." All banks that went bankrupt during that period (in record quantities) were just a variation of what happened here.

Does all this sound somewhat like the grocery store example that you read about earlier? If the owner and his family take groceries out the back door without paying for them he will probably go bankrupt. It happens in the banking business, too. Remember this, because in the banking system I am going to tell you about, you can also destroy it by not obeying the basic rules of banking. Loans have to be paid back or you can kill the best business in the world. It's up to you, but don't try to blame others when it happens.

You must admit that getting into the business this way is very costly and time consuming. It will be a long time before you show a profit—probably as much as ten years. But it must be extremely profitable over the long haul for people to go through the gory mess you have just read about. There is a much easier way to accomplish the creation of your own banking system and the mechanism has been around for over 200 years. It is tried and true. It is called *participating (i.e. dividend-paying) whole life insurance.* But the problem is that very few people know how the business works, including the home-office folks in the life insurance companies!

At this point, it will help if you understand what is meant by the word "co-generation." It is a term used in the production of electrical power. As most everyone knows electrical power is produced in plants using fossil fuels (coal and petroleum products), nuclear fuels or water to turn turbines. But there is another source of electrical power that is significant—the wood-products plants—sawmills and paper mills. Trees are harvested for the wood they contain but the bark on the outside of the tree and the sawdust from sawing lumber has little economic value, but they make a very good fire! This source of heat can do the same thing that fossil fuels do to turn dynamos to produce electricity. Every sawmill of significant size and all paper mills have a "co-generation plant" to make their own electricity.

Imagine that you own a paper mill and that your co-generation plant can produce 125% of your mill's need for electrical power. What do you do with the surplus power? Yes, you can sell it. But, do you erect power distribution lines, get a sales force, etc. and ask potential customers if they would like to buy power from you instead of their customary power supplier? Heavens, no! You understand how the power distribution systems all work and simply tie into the established system and sell *them* the power. It is much more efficient than trying to do it any other way. Creating your own banking system through the use of dividend-paying life insurance is much like co-generation. All the ingredients are *already there in place.* All you have to do is understand what is going on in such insurance plans and tap into the system.

CREATING YOUR OWN BANKING SYSTEM THROUGH DIVIDEND-PAYING LIFE INSURANCE

You should have put my money on deposit with the bankers so that when I returned I would have received it back with interest.
— Matthew 25:27

Banking—The business of a bank, originally restricted to money changing, and now devoted to taking money on deposit subject to check or draft, loaning money and credit and **any other associated form of general dealing in money or credit**.
— Webster's Third New International Dictionary

The very first principle that must be understood is that you *finance* everything that you buy—you either pay interest to someone else or you give up interest you could have earned otherwise. The alternate use of money must always be reckoned with. Some call this "opportunity cost." But, it is amazing how people give lip-service to this fact but do not put it into practice in their own financial dealings—the equivalent of thinking that the law of gravity applies to everyone else but them.

An excellent article appeared in the September 1993 issue of FORTUNE magazine, entitled "The Real Key To Creating Wealth" by Shawn Tully in which he describes the concept of Economic Value Added (EVA) developed by Stern Stewart & Co. of New York City. Tully says, "Understanding that while EVA is easily today's leading idea in corporate finance and one of the most talked about in business, it is far from the newest. On the contrary: Earning more than the cost of capital is about the oldest idea in enterprise. But just as Greece's glories were forgotten in the Dark Ages, to be rediscovered in the Renaissance, so the idea behind EVA has often been lost in ever darker muddles of accounting. Managers and investors who come upon it act as if they have seen a revelation."

In summary, before being introduced to EVA, corporations were borrowing capital from banks and paying interest—but they were treating their own capital (equity) *as if it had no cost!* When they were brought face-to-face with the error of their ways and conducted their business with this fact included in the equation, then the profitability increased dramatically. EVA's basic premise is—if you know what's really happening, you'll know what to do. The same thing applies to *The Infinite Banking Concept.*

In creating any product, it all begins with engineering. The automobile you drive started out being "lines on a piece of paper." If the production workers don't do what the engineers designed, you won't have an automobile, but they did, and your car rolls off the assembly line. Suppose that I get the next one and it is "identical" to yours—same color, equipment, features, etc.—they are identical in every way. Can you safely predict that they will both *perform identically* during their lifetimes? Of course not! Because you and I know someone that can get 200 to 300 thousand miles out of car with no trouble. But, we both know some people that can't get 50 thousand miles out of their car before it is "worn out!" How you drive the car and care for it is far more important than anything else. Keep this thought in mind as we look further at the life insurance product.

The engineers in life insurance are known as "actuaries." They are dealing with a field of 10 million selected lives—persons that have been through a screening process. And they are working with a theoretical life span of 100 years. Then they turn their information over to "rate makers" who determine what the company is going to have to charge its clients in order to be able to pay the death claims and make the whole system work over a long period of time.

Then the whole matter is turned over to lawyers who make legal and binding contracts that are to be offered to potential buyers through a sales force. The glue that holds this all together is comprised of the administrative folks, executives and clerks, etc. The contract is unilateral—that is, the company promises to do certain things if you meet the standards of acceptability and make premium payments. Read the contract and it will tell you very plainly that *you are the owner of the contract—not the company.* The Owner is the most important character in the scene.

To make the plan work the Owner must make payments into it and the Company (the hired-help) *must put the money to work* in order to produce the benefits that are promised. Those with the investment responsibility will do so in a number of ways—in financial instruments that are fairly conservative, e.g. bonds, mortgages, etc. Look at the investment portfolio of a number of life insurance companies and you will see what I mean. One place that is *speculative* that some companies *do* invest is in real estate developments and joint-ventures with other private organizations. Some large developments of urban office buildings have been entirely financed by a single insurance company. This can often include shopping centers.

But, upon reading the contract (the policy) you will find it plainly stated that the *Owner outranks every potential borrower in access to the money that must be lent!* And what he can borrow is 100% of his equity in the contract (the amount that the company can lend at any one time). If this is true—which it is—then what this amounts to is *absolute control* over the investment function of the company as it relates to the owner's policy. In essence, money can be lent to the other places *only if the Owner of the policy* does not exercise his option to use the money (and pay interest) instead.

As a result of the foregoing, there is an ever-increasing pool of money. From time to time an insured person dies. It doesn't happen very often—but when it does, the company pays the beneficiary from the pool of money and the cost of doing so is allocated among the policy owners on an equitable basis.

The "hired help," the administrators, must be paid for their work, too. You just can't run a business without "hired help." Just try to do it and see what happens. Your competitors that know better will run you out of business. This cost is also pro-rated among the policy owners, too.

At the end of the year the directors that actually run the company call the accountants in and, in essence, ask them, "How did we do this year on John Doe's policy in comparison with the assumptions made by the actuaries and the rate-makers in designing it?" We must digress at this point and remember that an actuary is a kind of engineer and that all engineers "overbuild" everything they design.

If he doesn't do so, he won't be an engineer very long! I think about this every time I get in the cockpit of an airplane. I have never seen an instrument panel that does not include an airspeed indicator with a red mark somewhere on the face of it. It is telling you, "Don't go past this point or the airplane will come apart on you, resulting in a rapid loss of control and imminent death to all occupants" or something to that effect. That is not true! It won't come apart until the airspeed is some 20 to 30 percent greater than the red mark. The engineers have put a "fudge factor" into the equation. But, if you operate the airplane just beyond the red line on a regular basis, you are putting stresses on the wings, etc. that are *cumulative* in their effects and one of these days you are going to reap the rewards of your actions. It won't be a pretty sight!

Furthermore, the policy is engineered to become more efficient every year, no matter what happens (that is, if the Owner does what is called for in premium paying, loan repayments plus interest thereon that are at least equal to or better than the general investment portfolio of the company). That is because the cash value is *guaranteed* to ultimately reach the face amount of the policy by age 100 of the Insured. There is an ever-decreasing "net amount at risk" for the company.

Not too many people are familiar with the concept of "getting better—no matter what," so let's look at the airplane world for help. Imagine that we are going to make a very long flight in a Boeing 747, so we load it with all the fuel that it will hold. This makes it capable of flying about 10,000 miles. By the time we fly 8,000 miles the airplane will now be able to do things that we would never attempt at takeoff. This is because we have burned up an enormous quantity of fuel and the airplane weighs that much less—but the engines are capable of producing as much power as when we took off. Therefore, every mile that we fly, the airplane will get more efficient—and you can't do a thing about it! It gets better—no matter what!

In designing the life insurance policy the rate-makers have taken into consideration the advice of the actuaries that their assumptions are *not* set in concrete. They include the interest earnings on the premiums paid by policy owners, the death claims expected during a time frame, and the expected cost of administration. Over a long period of time the actuaries can be pretty accurate, but from time to time the results can be better or worse than predicted. There are variations in interest earnings, death claims and expenses of operations and these factors affect the dividend scale declared for the coming year. You can safely say that the real results will *never* exactly match the illustration provided at the beginning of the life of a policy. But, once a dividend is declared, its value is *guaranteed* from that point on. It can *never* lose value in the future as can the value of securities. (It has always been a mystery to me, why do they call stocks *securities* when it is possible to lose their value entirely. It all sounds like an oxymoron to me. Maybe it is like Social Security, which has no market value at all?)

A significant period of *lower* than expected earnings of interest, or a period of *more* than expected death claims and/or administrative expenses can result in a "downer" for the company. When this happens in a regular corporation it is the function of the stock-holders to "take up the slack." But, in this case, the rate-makers are reminded that "*we don't have any stockholders*!" So, the rate-makers are cautioned by the actuaries that "if we calculate that it would require $1.00 per year for a given plan, don't collect $1.00—collect $1.10. This *extra* .10 is the *capital* that makes the whole system viable.

Now back to our scene on John Doe's policy—he has had it for a few years and the Directors have asked the accountants, "How did we do on John Doe's policy this year?" The accountants report that they had collected $1.10 but after calculating all the aforementioned factors they found that it took only 80 cents to deliver that promised death benefit in the future. This means the directors can make a decision with 30 cents. If they are "half-way" smart (and most of them are) they will take into consideration that they need to put a part of this into a *contingency fund* to prepare for unexpected future risks. So, they put .025 into the contingency fund and distribute .275 and call it a "dividend." Most people have the impression that this is a taxable event. This is not so. Remember that the Income Tax has only been with us since 1913 (the U.S. got along very well without it prior to that time; there were *surpluses* in the budget) and life insurance has been around for over 200 years. The word, *dividend* was used by the insurance industry to describe this dispersal and it stuck with us, but the correct classification is a *return of premium* (or a return of capital) which is not a taxable event in IRS terminology. If the owner uses the dividend to purchase Additional Paid-Up Insurance (no cost for acquisition, sales commissions, etc.) the result is an ever-increasing tax-deferred accumulation of cash values that support an ever-increasing death benefit. And there are no government bureaucrats looking over your shoulder telling you what you can and cannot do. The result is limited only by the imagination of the policy owner.

By the way, these dividends can get pretty significant over a long period of time. I bought a policy from a major insurance company in 1959 and the annual dividend is *over ten times* the annual premium now. They would have been much larger had I not used the annual dividend to *reduce premiums* for the first 15 years. These things are just not adequately explained by life insurance sales folks because of the limited understanding of their home office folks that teach them. A pity!

So far, this is pretty simple stuff. Now for the complicated part. The life insurance sales person calls on my "All-American young man" referred to earlier in this book (the one making $28,500 after taxes and is 29 years old) and urges him to consider "how much the world is going to miss you in the case of your untimely death." So he calculates his *human life value* by asking how much he expects to earn per year as an average and multiplies that by the number of years that he expects to work, assuming he lives that long. Assuming that he will get pay raises from time to time, it is reasonable that his average annual income to be something like $38,000 times 36 years (until his age 65) which will produce $1,368,000 in income. The insurance agent points out that he will use up something like 40% of this income stream to support his own needs. This means that $820,800 in income for his family and the charities he holds dear will vanish if he happens to die in the near future. To arrive at a principal sum (the capital that would be required to produce that income stream) this figure must be discounted at a nominal rate of interest. The agent says, "So, if we were to have to buy a machine that would produce that income to your family we would have to pay about $400,000 cash for the machine, NOW! That's how valuable you are to them and your charities. Mr. Doe, if you owned such a machine and it was subject to sudden loss of some kind, would you insure it?" Mr. Doe says, "By all means!" The agent asks, "How much would you insure it for?" "Why, $400,000, of course." To which the agent responds, "Ahh! Now that we have that established, let me show you *how little* you will have to pay *my company* to satisfy that need!"

My word! If you will take an honest look at what this young man is now doing — paying over 35% of every dollar of after-tax income to interest alone — it should be obvious that his *need for finance* is much greater than his *need for life insurance protection*. If he would solve for the need for finance through dividend-paying life insurance, he would *automatically* have much more life insurance *and recover all the interest he is now paying to someone else*. But this almost never occurs because of the mental block implanted by financial geniuses that "life insurance is a poor place to store money." What a limited outlook of just what is going on in the banking world! Again I remind you, if you know what's really happening, you'll know what to do.

And so, the young man puts $50 per month into life insurance premiums and feels that he is "insurance poor." He is worth more dead than alive, etc. Then he goes down to a dealer and buys an automobile, paying for it with a loan from a bank or finance company. Remember that there is only *one pool of money* out there in the world. The fact that any number of organizations or individuals are managing a portion of the pool is incidental. But, it can be even more specific when it comes to automobile loans; I have never seen a monthly list of investments from a dozen of major life insurance companies that did not include *finance companies* as a place where they have loaned blocks of money. The finance company simply buys blocks of money, adds a fee to it and loans it to consumers that buy cars. So, this man pays $260 per month for a minimum of 48 months for his $10,550 car loan. He does this throughout life because that's the way all his peers are doing it.

If he would take time out, and stand back far enough to get some perspective, he might notice that he is paying $50 per month into a pool of money (the life insurance policy) and paying $260 per month to an intermediary (the finance company that deducts a fee and lives *well* off the activity) which passes the residual sum back to the *same pool* of money! Furthermore, he complains about the premium he pays but thinks nothing of the much larger amount he pays the automobile finance company! Strange,

isn't it?

In the above example he is paying a total of $310 to the pool: $50 directly and $260 indirectly. If he could muster up the courage to pay the $310 *directly to the life insurance company* in the form of premiums for around four years, he could now make a policy loan and pay cash for the automobile!

Here comes the important part again, so pay close attention! The insurance agent now needs to make him *vividly* aware that he must *pay the loan back at an interest rate that is at least equivalent to the going interest rate of an automobile finance company*—not what the policy calls for. In this case it should be at least $260 per month. If the policyholder does this, then he will effectively *make* what the finance company would otherwise make and do it all on a tax-free basis. If the agent is really good, and understands the principles of banking, he will encourage the policyholder to pay $275 per month because the "extra" dollars will go to his policy to increase the capital that can be lent to other parties.

If the policyholder objects that, "it's my own money and I am not going to pay any interest at all"—or maybe, "I'm only going to pay 2.9% as seen in television commercials"—then the agent must remind him of the grocery store at the beginning of this book and explain it to him *one more time*! If he still doesn't understand then the agent needs to have him revisit the story of the failure of the First National Bank in Midland, Texas. If he still doesn't understand, the agent needs to resign from working with him because he is not teachable, and/or is a thief! Neither of these characters is a desirable business associate.

You have now had an explanation of all the essential principles of "banking" through the use of dividend-paying life insurance, but to understand the *infinite* qualities of *The Infinite Banking Concept* it requires a deeper look. In the above example of the car financing, the *capitalization* needs to be somewhat greater than just four years. Many college business professors estimate that corporations expect it to take at least seven years to get back a profit on a new investment. This is an understatement in certain undertakings. So, why not capitalize each policy purchased for *at least 7 years*, to the point where dividends will pay all the remaining premiums on the policy. (This will be explained in detail later on in the book). Would you have much of a grocery business if you were the only customer? You must build it to the point where you accommodate the needs of *others* in order to prosper. The same principle applies to banking.

Furthermore, I am not describing *one life insurance policy*. This is to be *a system of policies.* Have you not noticed that when a grocery store becomes successful in one location, then it tends to establish another store in another location? Have you not noticed that banks have branch offices? There must be a reason for their behavior! Then why not expand your own potential by buying all the life insurance on yourself that the companies will issue? And then on *all* the persons in which you have an insurable interest? At present, does not *all your income* go through the books of some banking institution? Don't the banks lend out the deposits of customers? All they do is *capitalize* the bank (Capital Stock) to make it a safe place for customers to deposit their money and then lend out the money left on deposit. If they don't lend money they will go out of business. It will take the average person *at least 20 to 25 years* to build a banking system through life insurance to accommodate all his own needs for finance—his autos, house, etc. But, once such a system is established, it can be passed on to future generations as long as they can be taught how the system works and suppress their baser instincts to "go out the back door of the grocery store"—or in a word that is more descriptive—*steal*.

BASIC UNDERSTANDINGS

YOU "FINANCE' everything you buy. You either pay interest to someone else or you give up interest you could have earned.

CREATE AN ENTITY— A plan — which you control and it makes money on your loans. One such entity can be a life insurance plan. Life insurance companies hire actuaries who design plans of insurance and then market those plans through agents. When someone buys one of these plans, the contract is very specific to point out who *owns* the plan (or policy). It is *not* the insurance company! The company is simply the administrator of the plan and must collect premiums—and *must* lend money out or make investments of one kind or another in order to be able to pay the death claims promised. Money is lent to any number of places and types of borrowers, including the owner of the policy if the owner so desires. The amount of money available to the owner is the entire equity in the policy at the time. In the hierarchy of places where money is lent, the owner ranks *first*. That is absolute CONTROL!

At the end of the year, the Life Insurance company makes an accounting of the experience that year of the death claims paid, the earnings on premiums collected, and the expenses of running the company. A dividend is declared which is actually a return to the policy owner of surplus premium that was collected. Hence, it is not an earning and, therefore, is not taxable. When that dividend is then used to buy additional paid-up insurance at cost, then the result is continuous compounding of an ever-increasing base.

It looks like this diagram:

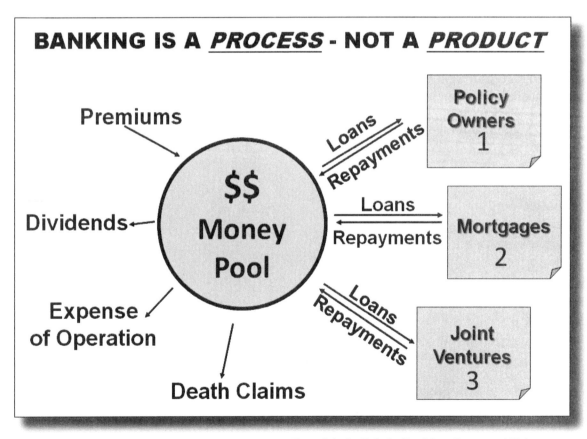

REVIEW - PART I

1. The importance of imagination -it is more important than knowledge.

   Gauss—child prodigy—didn't think like the others and made valuable contributions to the world. Can you add the numbers 1 through 1,000 in your head? (Answer: 500,500).

2. The grocery business. The value of learning how to get into a business in which you are a consumer of the same thing that you sell.

   It requires extensive study of the business prior to start-up. It requires very high capitalization.

   It requires extraordinary management abilities.

   When you shop for groceries at your store— don't steal, or your business will fail.

3. The money problem.

   Only money left over after paying taxes can be spent. For the average person in the U.S., 34.5% of that sum goes to pay interest, alone, to finance car purchases, homes, and various other purchases. This money is gone forever. It is making persons in the banking business wealthy. It can be yours to enrich your life forever—if you get into the banking business.

   Learn the importance of the Economic Value Added concept.

4. Creating a bank like the ones you already know about.

   It is much like getting in the grocery business - except much more difficult. It requires much more capital. You have to get a charter from the Commissioner. When you make loans to yourself at your bank - don't steal. You will destroy the best business in the world.

5. How a dividend-paying life insurance policy works.

   Review the diagram on page 26 and make sure that you understand the flow of money.

   In addition, make sure you understand "the characters in the play" (see Glossary in the back of this book). The policyholder is the principal character in every life insurance policy.

6. The capitalization phase.

   It is going to take time and discipline for several years. Don't expect to get rich overnight. But the rewards, later on, are worth all the effort.

PART II - THE HUMAN PROBLEMS - UNDERSTANDING PARKINSON'S LAW

Thus far, we have covered only the technical aspects of creating your own banking system through dividend-paying life insurance. Now, we must face *the human problems.*

C. Northcote Parkinson, (1909-1993), was a British essayist, lecturer, and economist who left us with some valuable writings of his observations. One of the best is his little book *Parkinson's Law,* in which he brilliantly isolates some of the limitations of us all, particularly the behavior of individuals within a group. He makes one painfully aware of the futility of expecting good results from committees! He reminds me of a sign at a church that read, "God so loved the world that *He did not send a committee."*

In *Parkinson's Law* he says, "work expands to meet the time envelope allowed." Check it out—give a person a job to do and give a time limit of three days to complete it. You can bet the grocery money that it won't get done until *late on the third day!* Now assign *the same job* but allow thirty days for its completion—and you should not be surprised that it is finished *late on the 30th day!*

He also noted that "a luxury, once enjoyed, becomes a necessity." Can you remember when we did not have air-conditioned automobiles? Would you think of buying one *without air-conditioning?* Not me!

And he said, "expenses rise to equal income." Is it true? Income is limited for us all, but our wishes far exceed our ability to fund them. When a pay raise comes along it is very quickly absorbed by *a new definition of necessities!!*

It doesn't have to be this way—but it is!! Parkinson's Law must be overcome *daily.* If you cannot do so then just go ahead and give up—you are destined to become a slave! That's the bad news. The good news is—if you *can* whip Parkinson's Law you will *win by default* because your peers can't do it—and everything you do in the financial world is compared with what they are doing. In all our efforts at establishing priorities we should begin with a thorough consideration of the truth of *Parkinson's Law.*

Parkinson once told a story about a British government official who served at the time of World War I. Young civil servants used to bustle into his office waving documents, emphasizing the high priority of this and the top secrecy of that. He would listen patiently and tell each young person to leave his paper on the desk. Then, as the youth reached the door, he would call out: "Oh, one thing." "Sir?" "Remember Rule Six." "Yes sir, of course." The young worker would reach the door and then turn back, having had another thought. "But excuse me, sir. What is Rule Six?"

"Rule Six is as follows: Don't take yourself too seriously." Once more the youth would be at the door with his hand on the doorknob and would turn again as a new idea struck him. "But sir," he would ask, "what are the other rules?" "Young man," would come the reply, "there are no other rules."

WILLIE SUTTON'S LAW

We have looked at Parkinson's Law and *if you can* overcome it you will win by default in comparison with your peers because they can't do it! Now you must face Willie Sutton's Law. I remind you that Willie Sutton (1901-1980), was a notorious bank robber in our nation's history. When asked why he continued to rob banks he replied, "That's where they keep the money." So Sutton's Law is formulated thusly—**wherever wealth is accumulated someone will try to steal it**. Willie did not invent this activity; he was just a stellar practitioner of the art as an individual. The phenomenon has been with us since the beginning of time. Theft was the first labor-saving idea—don't produce anything, just *steal* that which someone else has produced!

Question: Who is the biggest thief in the world? If you answered the Internal Revenue Service you are correct! Most people have this feeling but lack the ability to explain that it is indeed, theft. I explain it this way. Let's go to a shopping mall or some such place where there are lots of people to witness what I am about to do to you. At this point I pull out a gun and place it against your head and direct you to "give me the contents of your wallet or I will blow your brains out!" I can predict with certainty that those who saw this act will describe it as *theft*—and call for my punishment. But—if you will allow me to gather that same crowd for about an hour before you show up—and let me talk to them about how we are going to divide the contents of your wallet and distribute *among them*—now they will call the act "*democracy in action!*"

Frederic Bastiat (1801-1850), a French economist and statesman who wrote an essay entitled *The Law* in 1850 states it this way:

> "*The law perverted! And the police powers of the state perverted along with it! The law, I say, not only turned from its proper purpose but made to follow an entirely contrary purpose! The law become the weapon of every kind of greed! Instead of checking crime, the law itself guilty of the evils it is supposed to punish! If this is true, it is a serious fact, and moral duty requires me to call the attention of my fellow-citizens to it.*"

What Bastiat saw in France in the mid-1800s, and which we have in super abundance currently in the United States, he correctly identified as *legal plunder!* He goes on to explain, "But how is this legal plunder to be identified? Quite simply: See if the law takes from some persons what belongs to them, and gives it to other persons to whom it does not belong. See if the law benefits one citizen at the expense of another by doing what the citizen himself cannot do without committing a crime."

As a result of the above bit of history you will find yourself engulfed in confiscatory taxation if you are the least bit effective in producing and accumulating wealth. You can count on it! Willie Sutton's Law is active! At this point there are many that resort to despair—but there is no need for it. The government lawmakers and bureaucrats who carry out these perversions of law fully understand that they are dealing with a *parasite-host* relationship. Government is not capable of producing anything—it gets all its sustenance from the productive element of society. Government is a *parasite* and lives off the productive taxpayers, *the host.* It is self-evident that if the parasite takes all the produce of the host, then *both parties die!!* Government officials may be cunning—but they are not stupid! (But immediately I remind myself that the USSR did exactly that! They shot themselves through the heart.)

When taxation becomes onerous to the point where government officials sense rebellion they always resort to *exceptions to the rule.* They invented *qualified* pension plans, HR-10 plans, 401-K plans, IRAs, etc., ad nauseam. What a classic case of *appointing the fox to guard the chicken house!* How totally absurd! Did you also notice that all these plans were not installed simultaneously? First it was pension plans which "blessed" one select group of citizens, and then HR-10 plans for another group, etc. Finally it came down to IRAs so that *everyone has an exception to the rule!* Can you believe it! The lawmakers create a problem by spending money that they do not have which results in strangling taxation—and then they create a "solution" in the form of *an exception to the rules they created!* The natural result of such a process is a system in which the government *controls* everything you do—and they *can, and will, change their mind* upon the slightest whim of the times. And they keep changing the rules so that it looks like they are trying to "help you out." The *real solution* is to quit the government spending for all the "programs" and get out of the lives of the citizens. But at every turn you see "Financial Planners" and writers that label themselves as various kinds of "financial experts" who, without exception, recommend that you should "participate to the fullest extent possible in your tax-sheltered programs." It is self-evident that these programs would disappear if there were no willing participants.

I remind you that the thing that caused all of this burden is the Income Tax Law which did not exist, as we know it, until 1913. Before then our country had surpluses in the national budget and the world got along very well. But after its adoption the American public now noted that it could "vote itself a benefit through its Representatives in Washington – and send the bill to everyone else." Such behavior will naturally lead to the mess that we wrestle with now.

> *There are two methods, or means, and only two, whereby man's needs and desires can be satisfied: One is the production and exchange of wealth; this is the economic means. The other is the uncompensated appropriation of wealth produced by others; this is the political means... The State is the organization of the political means.*
> —Albert J. Nock, *Our Enemy, The State*

> *The State is that great fiction whereby everyone tries to live at the expense of everyone else.*
> —Frederic Bastiat

We all need to protect ourselves from the devastating effects of this monstrous idea outlined above. It just can't work. Yet, generation after generation keeps trying the same old nonsense. Economic problems are best solved by people freely contracting with one another and with government limited to the function of enforcing those contracts. And the best way to do so is through the magnificent idea of *dividend-paying whole life insurance!* It has been around for over 200 years. It has stood the test of time. It is not compulsory. *It is not a government-sponsored idea!* It preceded the income tax idea by a long time. It is *private property!* And only the people who care about others that are dear to them participate in the idea. What a great group of people to be associated with in business!

THE GOLDEN RULE

The Golden Rule— *Those who have the Gold make the rules!*

We all have the tendency to chuckle when we see this perversion of a principle that was learned in childhood, one that serves us very well, that we should do unto others as we would have them do unto us! But this corruption is *very true, also!* I think that it is a pity that it is not often looked upon with favor. Perhaps it is because we have almost lost the concept of what capitalism is all about. The common man has become so infatuated with living for today that the importance of saving—of creating capital—is all but a lost value. The American savings rate is miserably low. At the time of this writing it has been *negative!* Last month it was at an all-time low.

As a result someone else must provide the capital that is necessary to sustain our way of life. This strategy carries with it a very high cost, and we all suffer the consequences. It all begins with faulty premises.

Let me build the case this way. What could be more idyllic than a marriage of Japanese capital and Mexican labor? Here we have one group of people who need employment in the worst way - and there is another group that has more money than you can imagine! If we can only get them together on a project it would be paradise!!

A few years back Panasonic wanted to build a plant in Mexico to solve the obvious equation. But in the *infinite wisdom of the Mexican government* at that time, if you wanted to establish such a business there, they required that *Mexicans should own 51% of the business.* That means that Mexicans control the business.

The typical Japanese strategy runs something like this—you put money into a business and you should *expect to lose money for five years.* When you start making money you should plow it all back into the business *for five more years.* Only after this time should you expect to take money out of the business. But the typical Mexican outlook on a business venture is *to demand a bonus at the very start*—like a signing bonus for a star athlete, etc.!!

Do I have to tell you what happened? Panasonic pulled out of Mexico and went somewhere else where capital is appreciated and managed with care. Who won and who lost in this story? Panasonic *had the Gold,* and so they *made the rules*!! It can be no other way. Capital is a responsibility and should be treated with great respect. If not, then all parties involved will lose. It is really difficult to write or talk about this fact, perhaps because it is so blatantly obvious!! When you have a large amount of cash on hand all sorts of good opportunities *will appear,* and you can also negotiate very favorable purchase prices. So many of life's problems would disappear if this understanding was generally accepted *and practiced widely* among the population. A word of caution is in order, do not think that *everyone* must conduct his financial affairs in this manner. It is not a numbers game. Individuals can reap the rewards that such discipline yields. In fact, we all need to remind ourselves that *whatever you do in the financial world is compared with what everyone else is doing.*

Then, why is there general despair in our country regarding financial matters? Why are people "paying through the nose" for capital? Why the feelings of helplessness and futility? I say again, it all begins with *faulty premises.*

Let me try to explain it this way. I was recently re-reading a piece that Jackson Pemberton wrote back in 1976 entitled, "A New Message on the Constitution." (I am assuming that there is general agreement that we face monumental problems in our country, at present which, can easily destroy us). Pemberton is writing as if he was one of the "Founding Fathers" involved in construction of the Constitution and is pointing out where successive generations have gone astray.

"—but in spite of all our careful effort, we knew that it was not sufficient to merely launch the ship of state correctly, it needed to be tended by an alert, informed, and jealous citizenry. But history, like nature, travels in cycles; both liberty and

oppression contain the seeds of their own destruction. Our success has brought the security which put you to sleep.”

Now, basking in the dimming brilliance of the lights of liberty, you have been neither vigilant nor informed, and only recently have you begun to realize the correctness of your rising jealousy for your rights. Let those feelings of jealousy well up within you and cause you to alert yourselves to your true condition.

Your executives have taken upon themselves to form foreign alliances and make domestic regulations without proper authority. They have violated your most fundamental law. Your judiciary has ignored the amending process and altered the meaning and intent of the Constitution they were sworn to defend. They have betrayed your most fundamental law. Your Congress has been watchful, yet not of the encroachments of the other two branches, but for opportunity to gain influence *by purchasing your favor with your own money*. They have ignored your most fundamental law. And you—you — seek for a remedy while it stares you in the face! You have lost the vision of your most fundamental law. Let me show you. You call the national charter 'the Constitution of the United States,' and that simple phrase contains both the totality of your plight and the seeds of your salvation; for in those six words you reveal your feeling that both you and your law are subject to your government. You are not the slave of government at all, but *because you think so*, you may as well be! Nay! The Constitution is *your* servant and the master of your government. It is not the Constitution of the United States, it is the Constitution *of the people,* and *for* the United States! It is not only the law by which you are governed, it is the law by which *you may govern your government!* It is not the law by which high-handed politicians may impose their collective will upon you, it is for you to impose it upon them! It does not belong to the government, it belongs

to you! It is yours! It is yours to enforce upon your government! It is yours to read to those self-wise do-gooders; and if you will hold it high in your hand, they will quail and flee before it like the cowardly knaves they are, while those who are your true friends will rejoice in your new commitment.”

This explains what I mean when I say, “Most people know there is a play going on out in the world—but they don't understand it. Worse than that, they can't get the characters in the play straight!” (Recalling that Shakespeare said, “All the world is a stage and the people are the actors thereon”). People just don't play their proper role in the scheme of things. They have abdicated their opportunity/responsibility as it pertains to the banking function in the economy. They are depending on someone else to perform that job—and that character in the play is *making most of the money*! And rightly so, because of the Golden Rule—*those who have the gold make the rules!* It can be no other way!

To further compound the problem, there is this prevailing tendency in the current crop of Americans to look to government solutions to what they think is a problem that is outside themselves. “I don't have any money to buy a home (go to college, buy food, endure an emergency, care for my health, maintain the lifestyle that I desire, etc.) so there should be some sort of government program to provide these things for me. I have a right to them!”

Bureaucrats, elected officials, teachers in government schools, some members of the clergy, political action committees, media people, and there is no telling how many other such groups I have left out, foster this kind of thinking at every turn. It is a national disease—and to survive in the future this disease must be overcome. You just can't think that way and succeed.

Succumbing to these feelings produces a huge burden on your financial future—the price must be paid. You will always be at the mercy of the ones who have the gold! Further amplification of this factor will be given later in the book in the chapter entitled *The Cost of Acquisition*.

Ayn Rand, in her tremendous novel, *Atlas Shrugged*, isolates the results of this type of thinking perfectly. It is a long book—some 1,100 pages—but it is well worth the reading.

THE ARRIVAL SYNDROME

 Now we turn our attention to probably the most devastating matter that we have examined thus far—I call it "The Arrival Syndrome." This phenomenon probably limited the achievements of mankind more than anything else. When this "thing" infects us, we stop growing, stop learning. We ROT! We turn off or tune out the ability to receive inspiration — because we "already know all there is to know!"

Remember Ed Deming (1900-1993), that wonderful business consultant who was still working at age 93! He was the person who taught the Japanese the idea of quality. Business schools all over our country fell in love with his teachings—*after the Japanese showed the world the results.* But shortly after World War II, Ed started trying to get the attention of American businesses and teach them his ideas. Almost without exception Ed ran into the response, *"But we are already doing that."* No, they were not *doing that!* They were only taking a superficial look at what Ed was saying and jumping to the conclusion that they already understood all ramifications of Ed's concept. And so, Ed turned to Japan, with an economy that was non-existent—they were flat on their backs—and he found a culture that already knew discipline, and was willing to listen and *do what he said.* The rest is history and American manufacturers paid the price for their arrogance. When Ed came back to America much later he was accepted as being a genius. Many business schools in America now sing the praises of Ed Deming.

Daniel Boorstin (1914-2004), the historian, stated it this way, "The greatest obstacle to discovering the shape of the earth, the continents, and the oceans was not ignorance—it was the *illusion of knowledge.*"

As practitioners of teaching clients to develop their own Banking Systems *this* is probably our hardest job—to get people to open up their minds and take an in-depth look at just exactly what is going on in the business world and correctly classify what is seen. A quote from the EVA article in FORTUNE magazine in September 1993 comes to mind, *"If you understand what's really happening, you'll know what to do."*

Disturb us O Lord when we are too well pleased with ourselves, when our dreams have come true because we dreamed too little, when we arrived safely because we sailed too close to the shore.

Disturb us O Lord, when with the abundance of things we possess we have lost our thirst for the waters of life; having fallen in love with life, we have ceased to dream of eternity. And in our efforts to build a new earth, we have allowed our vision of the new Heaven to dim.

Disturb us, O Lord, to dare more boldly, to venture on wider seas where storms will show your mastery; where losing sight of land, we shall find the stars.

We ask you to push back the horizons of our hopes; and to push us in the future in strength, courage, hope and love.

This we ask in the name of our Captain, who is Jesus Christ.

- Sir Francis Drake's prayer before he set out to be the first man to circumnavigate the world. Portsmouth, England 1577

You may say to yourself, "My power and the strength of my hands have produced this wealth for me." But remember the LORD our God, for it is he who gives you the ability to produce wealth, and so confirms his covenant, which he swore to your forefathers, as it is today.

- Deuteronomy 8:17-18

USE IT OR LOSE IT

Mark 4:25 - *For he that hath, to him shall be given: and he that hath not, from him shall be taken even that which he hath.*

In our look at the Basic Understandings as taught by *The Infinite Banking Concept* we come to the last of the human considerations which must be faced if we are to be successful in becoming our own banker. This thought is closely allied to the one we looked at last, "The Arrival Syndrome."

Please note that all the points that we have addressed so far—Parkinson's Law, Willie Sutton's Law, The Golden Rule, The Arrival Syndrome, and now, Use It or Lose It—have to do with *overcoming human nature.* All human progress is predicated on this matter. It is not easy to conquer but it is absolutely necessary. It is like recognizing the fact that we must attend to bodily hygiene or face the consequences. Don't brush your teeth regularly and they will rot!

The Arrival Syndrome produces a "comfort zone" that causes people to lapse into their old way of doing things—a lifetime of accumulated information that determines how one conducts oneself. The fact that this conclusion may be based on fallacious information is beside the point! I illustrate the point by telling people, "what I'm teaching is equivalent to teaching that the *world is round*—when most folks think that it is *flat.* Technically, that is a very simple thing to explain—but if you are one of those who think it is flat, then it becomes a very difficult problem!" The Infinite Banking Concept is dealing with a totally different paradigm. This amounts to a personal *monetary system.*

In the September 1993 issue of FORTUNE magazine the story of economic value added (EVA) was reported. Many large corporations had achieved phenomenal success when they adopted EVA. All the concept amounts to is the recognition of the fact that your own capital has a cost of money as well as that which has been borrowed from banks. That is the *very first point* made in The Infinite Banking Concept "Basic Understandings" page in the workbook.

Among those corporations featured was Coca Cola, who, by the way, was on the cover of the March 1996 issue of FORTUNE as "the most admired company in America."

A follow-up story in FORTUNE in May 1995 was titled, "EVA WORKS - -BUT NOT IF YOU MAKE THESE COMMON MISTAKES." The points made looked like this:

- They don't make it a way of life.
- Most managers try to implement EVA too fast.
- The boss lacks conviction.
- Managers fuss too much.
- Training gets short shrift.

Accepting a totally new point of reference means that one must develop new habits. In talking with members of the Infinite Banking Concept think tank we continue to notice that many are still caught up in the posture of thinking that the matter is a function of *interest rates.* This is a fatal error. It has to do with recognizing where money is flowing to and the failure of charging interest to yourself for the things that you buy using your own banking system. Anytime that you can cut out the payment of interest to others and direct that *same market rate of interest* to an entity that you own and control, which is subject to minimal taxation (life insurance companies *do pay taxes*), then you have improved your situation.

Just like EVA, to be effective, The Infinite Banking Concept must become a way of life. *You must use it or lose it*!

CREATING THE ENTITY

In designing Life Insurance policies, the beginning point is the work of actuaries, the engineers of the whole process. They are working with a mortality table that is constructed from data on ten million *selected* lives—people that have been through a selection process—not the "person off the street." The purpose of the selection process is to prevent *adverse selection against the company,* that is, to cull out those persons who are facing predictable death in the near future. It would not be a good thing for all the people insured to include persons that have a terminal illness, that are contemplating suicide, etc. Cancer patients and people with heart disease fall in the same category. And they are working with a theoretical life span of 100 years.

The graphical illustration of the 1958 Commissioner's Standard Ordinary Mortality Table is illustrated here. There have been later editions of Mortality Tables, but it doesn't matter all that much *when* the tables were constructed because the final result of the situation is dependent on the earnings of the money invested by the company, the current mortality experience of the

company, and the expense of operating the company. All they need is a field of data from which to begin calculations. If mortality experience is better than that indicated by the mortality table, then it will reflect that fact by *better dividends* distributed to the policyholders. In fact, the substantial increase in dividends paid by companies can be attributed mostly to better mortality experience in the past several decades.

Note that only 100 out of the original 1,000 have died by age 45, and out of those remaining, 75% are still alive at age 65! Can you guess what has happened to life expectancy since 1958? Yes, there has been a significant increase in longevity! By the way, do you know where all this business of *retirement at age 65* came from? Franklin D. Roosevelt got it from Bismarck in Germany several years earlier. The whole idea was to "get these old folks out of the work force in order to provide jobs for the younger generation," as if there are only so many jobs around—a socialist mental hang-up that has no validity at all.

From all that I can determine life expectancy for males in America in 1937 was 61 years. Now the figure is in the mid-70s—*but we are still using age 65 for retirement purposes.* The coming debacle of

---

OUT OF 1,000 AMERICANS BORN .... 1,000 DIE!

DIE PRIOR TO AGE 21

-AGE 25

OUT OF 900 ALIVE AT 45

-AGE 45

¼ WILL DIE DURING THEIR PRIME WORKING YEARS

-AGE 65

¾ WILL REQUIRE INCOME AFTER 65

-AGE 80

¼ WILL REQUIRE INCOME AFTER 80

-AGE 100   You are looking at the 1958 CSO Mortality Table

Social Security is the natural result of operating from a faulty premise.

It is not going to work! There is no legitimate reason for using such fallacious thinking to plan your life. [I once read that John Templeton, creator of *The Templeton Fund* who "retired" at age 80 and is now doing only charitable work (and working harder than ever) made the observation that *all should plan on working to at least age 70* before considering retirement]. The most productive years are being wasted.

Study the mortality charts and notice where most all of the dying takes place. Out of the 900 alive at age 45, seventy-five percent of them die past age 65. Of course, the situation is much more accentuated toward later deaths now. But in the everyday conversations about the "need" for life insurance, it is all centered on the period of age 21 to age 65. Not many people die during this period.

In creating plans of purchasing life insurance, all calculations by the rate-makers begin with the cost, *in a single sum*, of providing a plan of insurance that would cover one for the whole of life. It is called *single premium life insurance.* The insured plunks down the single sum and insurance is guaranteed for the rest of his life. It is possible to buy life insurance this way, but it is not a common occurrence.

The diagram on page 38 is a continuum that depicts all the different purchase plans. On the left end of the scale is single premium insurance. On the extreme right side is *term insurance.* In this plan the insured is *simply renting* the single premium insurance for a limited period of time. When life insurance began (over 200 years ago) it was *all* term insurance! It paid a death benefit *if* the insured died during the given time frame. So the insured persons paid ever-increasing premiums (because each year they lived it was more probable that they would die in the current year) and finally quit because the premiums became prohibitive—and a few years later, they died!

Perceptive people noticed that this was not like other forms of *insurance.* They buy fire insurance and it pays a benefit *if* a fire occurred during the period covered. They buy accident insurance and it pays a benefit *if* an accident occurred during the period covered. There is a very strong probability that *neither of the above would ever occur*! But death

for a person is not an *if*—it is a *when!* Responding to pressures from the market place, life insurance companies created a plan for purchasing the single premium policy with a payment period that began with the current age of the insured and extending to the theoretical life span of 100 years. They called the plan *ordinary life.* I submit that this was a gross misnomer! When you classify something it is based on its major characteristics. The "animal" they created had much more in common with banking than it did with life insurance. When you look at the proportions of the whole activity it is obvious that the *banking qualities* became much greater than the death benefit quality of a policy. A better name would have been "a banking system with a death benefit thrown in for good measure."

The whole idea of *The Infinite Banking Concept* started with the realization that there is a huge amount of nonsense going on in the market place because of the misclassification of things. This is not new, nor is it unique to the financial world. For instance, take the case of the common potato. In the late 1500's the Conquistadors of Spain were down in South America (in what is now Peru) looking for gold. They didn't find much gold but they did find a plant that they took back to Europe. It was the potato! But no one in Europe would have anything to do with the plant because the botanists of the time *correctly identified the plant* as one from the plant family, *Solanaceae.* This family has a large number of poisonous plants in it, such as *Deadly Nightshade, Jimson weed,* etc. Because of this relationship it was thought that the potato was poisonous, also. (By the way, the *sprouts and the green parts* of the potato plant *are* poisonous! Don't eat them or you can develop serious gastric disorders.)

From the family *Solanaceae* also comes *belladonna,* a valuable medicine. It is from the leaves of the belladonna plant that we get atropine. Small quantities do marvelous things for the digestive tract—but in large quantities it can kill you! All medicines are poisonous!

The strange thing is that the Europeans went from a condition of thinking that the potato was *poisonous* to one of large-scale *dependence* on it. Remember that the Irish experienced mass starvation as a result of the potato famine when a blight wiped out the crop repeatedly. Of course, this change of understanding took place over a long period of time.

The world seems to always behave that way! We pick up some screwball idea that is based on a half-truth and let it grow into a monster that blinds us to what is really happening.

By the way, *the value of one year's crop of potatoes in the world now exceeds the value of all the gold found in the Western Hemisphere!* So the Spaniards *really did find gold* in Peru—but it wasn't in the form that they were expecting!

or loan is made. It is not a matter of earth-shaking consequences, but it can be avoided with a little bit of understanding of just what is going on. So, why bother with getting on the left side of the MEC line? After all, we are not attempting to accomplish all of the banking needs through the device of *one policy*— we will need a *system of many policies* in order to do the complete job. This is just a description of the design for each policy to best accomplish the system.

When using this type of life insurance to solve

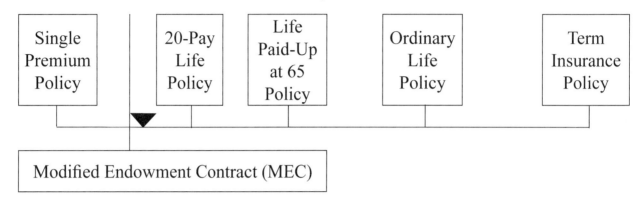

The tomato plant came to us from Mexico and it, too, suffered from the same misunderstanding. Thomas Jefferson introduced the tomato to the dinner table in America although most everyone considered it to be poisonous. If you have figured out that it also comes from the plant family *Solanaceae* then go to the head of the class!

Returning to the scale of policies above, suppose that the insured was 25 years old—then the *ordinary life* policy would be a 75-pay plan. The payment plan could be shortened by buying a *life paid-up at age 65* (for the same 25 year old, this would be a 40-pay plan). It could be further shortened to a 30-pay plan, or a 20-pay plan. *The shorter the payment period the better suited it is for the purposes of the Infinite Banking Concept.*

Notice the triangle at the bottom of the scale of various plans. Any plan located to the left of this line is classified by the Internal Revenue Service as a Modified Endowment Contract (or MEC). These plans are not treated as life insurance by the IRS, meaning that any *withdrawal or loan* from the plan would be treated as a distribution and would be taxed as from any other accumulation account, i.e., part is capital and part is earnings. The *earnings* portion is taxed as ordinary income in the year the withdrawal

your need for banking, it is best to select a plan (the base policy) that is in the middle of the scale (such as ordinary life or a life paid-up at age 65) and add a Paid-Up Additions Rider (PUA) to the plan. By varying the amount allocated to each portion you can place the resultant policy at any point between the base policy and the MEC line. The whole idea is to "snuggle up to the MEC line"—but don't cross it! This will de-emphasize the immediate death benefit but accentuate the banking qualities (the cash values). The irony is that doing it this way will result in providing *more* death benefit at the point where death will *probably* occur than any other plan! The base policy will pay dividends and the PUA rider will also pay dividends. These should be used to buy *Additional Paid-Up Insurance,* which gives more meaning to the *infinite* qualities of the system.

In describing this design of a policy, some people have called the process of putting a Paid-Up Additions rider on an ordinary life policy "over-funding" the policy. Maybe that can help in the overall understanding, but the objective should be simply to get *as much money as possible* into a policy with the *least amount of insurance* instead of trying to put as little money in and provide the greatest amount of insurance (initially). It is the exact opposite of what one thinks about when purchasing "insurance." This is understandable because of the history of how the whole subject developed.

It all reminds me of things such as when Christopher Columbus started his journey Westward from Europe to get to the East; his destination in particular, was India. When his party finally arrived at some islands in the Caribbean they met some people they had never seen before. They called them INDIANS! They *weren't*—but the name stuck. There are probably thousands of such examples of misclassification that we run into every day but they probably don't increase the quality of our lives. Instead, they limit our thinking and lead us to wrong conclusions. Words are powerful things!

MY THOUGHTS ON UNIVERSAL LIFE AND VARIABLE LIFE

Universal Life was invented in the early 1980s by E. F. Hutton, a stock brokerage firm that, in my opinion, knew nothing about life insurance. Remember the television commercial, "When E. F. Hutton speaks, everyone listens." Have you heard him say anything lately? They don't exist anymore! UL was nothing more than "one-year term insurance with a side fund of an interest-bearing account." It was an attempt to "un-bundle" the savings element and the life insurance element of a whole life policy—something that can't be done, if one understands the concept of whole life insurance.

This happened during a time of high interest rates and it "looked good" in the early years of the policy. When I first saw the policy I ran some illustrations and they kept "falling apart" when the insured attained age 65 to 70. The cost of one-year term became prohibitive at the advanced ages and "ate up the cash fund" from that point forward. Therefore, I never sold one of them when I was in the business—and I surely wouldn't buy one!

Next came Executive Life out in California. They made a "big splash" in the business and ultimately went broke. I understand that policy owners actually lost money with their policies.

Does the name, Michael Milken, mean anything to you? He did prison time as a result of his financial shenanigans. Would you guess where he was selling all of those "junk bonds?" If you replied, "Executive Life," then go to the head of the class! Would you like your financial future in the hands of people like that?

Lastly, there came Variable Life, invented by Equitable Life Assurance Society. It was nothing more than one-year term insurance with a side fund of a mutual fund. There are more mutual funds than there are stocks. No mutual fund is any better than its manager. The great preponderance of mutual fund managers had never seen a down-turn in the market until the recent one.

I suggest that you read *The Truth About Mutual Funds*. Then read *The Battle for the Soul of Capitalism* by John Bogle, the originator of The Vangard Fund. These two books are vital to the understanding of what goes on in that industry. Also read *The Pirates of Manhattan* by Barry Dyke. Upon completion of these three books you should be adequately informed to make an intelligent decision as to whether you should consider Variable Life.

I was with Equitable Life when Variable Life came on the scene. I never sold one of those policies— and I would never buy one. I do not recommend its use for the *Infinite Banking Concept*.

The tragedy of our times is that the life companies never spent any time on understanding Dividend-paying Whole Life Insurance and teaching the buying public its characteristics.

REVIEW - PART II

1. Pitfalls of human behavior.

   Make sure that you fully understand all five of these factors. They are "bedrock" in building your banking business. For instance, if you can't whip Parkinson's Law, then don't bother to read further. You are wasting your time and you are doomed to slavery.

2. Understand the mortality graph that the actuaries in life insurance companies must work with.

   Life expectance has increased dramatically during the last century.

   For banking purposes you want the highest cost life insurance that is possible, but avoid it becoming a Modified Endowment Contract. Minimize the death benefit and maximizing the cash value.

3. In a dividend-paying life insurance policy, you earn both guaranteed cash value, (interest) and dividends, which are not guaranteed and are based upon the experience of the company. In a well-managed company, the dividends can become enormous over a long period of time.

PART III - HOW TO START BUILDING YOUR OWN BANKING SYSTEM

When recalling the mountain of interest that "the All-American Man" is paying as depicted on page 17, one tends to look at the huge amount being paid to the mortgage on his house and concludes, "that is where I should start because it is such a significant drain on my situation." No, that one is overwhelming and would involve such a radical change in lifestyle that it becomes practically impossible. It is much better to attack an area that is attainable in a fairly short time—try the one about financing automobiles.

There are five legitimate methods of having the use of an automobile over the lifetime of a person. The following graph assumes that the car will be replaced at four-year intervals and that the "financing package" each time will be $10,550 at 8.5% interest for 48 months and we will be looking at a 44 year time frame in which to compare the results of the methods.

METHOD A—The FIRST, and most expensive method, is to lease the cars each year for 44 years. It is somewhat difficult to calculate the total cost in this case. We must resort to logic and reason and use the second method as a starting point. At the end of each 4 year period the lessee has no equity to show for the expenditure.

METHOD B—The SECOND method is using a commercial bank (or finance company) to do the job. Calculating the cost in this example is simple ($260 per month for 528 months = $137,280). At the end of each 4 year period, this person has a 4 year old car to use as a trade-in on the next unit. Reason tells you that the first method *must be more costly* than this one. Otherwise, no one would ever purchase— they would all *lease.* This would be absurd. One must lease from an *owner* who had to buy the car. Is the owner a fool? Is he not going to make some money on the activity? Therefore, let's assign an arbitrary 44 year cost of method one at $175,000. By the way, the annual equivalent of $260 per month is $3,030.

METHOD C—The THIRD method is to pay cash for each new car every four years. This results in a total cost of $116,050 ($10,550 for each trade-in times 11 cars). This person had to *defer* the use of the first new car for four years to achieve this result. He had to save up money for the first four years and immediately start accumulating money again in the same savings account to prepare for the next purchase. This method involves *car payments* just like the first two methods. It is all a matter of where

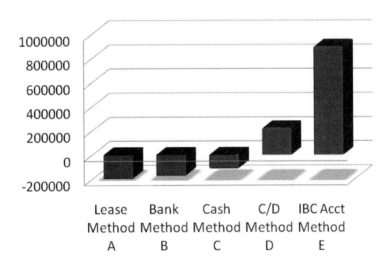

Figure 1

Five methods of having use of an automobile over a forty-four year period of time

(bar chart, y-axis from -200000 to 1000000; categories: Lease Method A, Bank Method B, Cash Method C, C/D Method D, IBC Acct Method E)

the payments are made—to the leasing company, the commercial bank, or to his savings account. This is the classical *sinking fund* method of financing the ongoing need for something. Notice that there is not much difference between the three methods discussed thus far. Also, be aware that we have probably covered 90% of all the population of the U.S. in the first three methods. It should be noted, too, that we are "going the right way" on the graph as we move to the right on the scale of methods—but mid-stream America is going the other way! Leasing is up 35% in the last few years, according to many radio commercials.

METHOD D—The FOURTH method requires some explanation. The first three methods have not addressed the need for *capitalization*; a pool of money must be accumulated before using it for your own car purchases and it must be large enough to accommodate the needs of some other folks, too. Remember the grocery store described earlier. If the grocery store is only large enough to serve only your own needs, you won't have much of a successful business. Several years ago Dartmouth Business Professor, James Bryan Quinn, estimates that corporations expect it to take at least seven years to get back a profit on a new investment. Taking a clue from this fact, why not accumulate money over a *seven-year* period of time and at a somewhat higher annual amount, say $5,000.

This person accumulates money on a monthly basis in a savings account and buys a Certificate of Deposit (at someone else's bank) in the amount of $5,000 with a yield of 5.5% interest. Show me someone that will do this for seven years just to build a banking system and I will show you someone that has conquered Parkinson's Law. He will win by default in comparison with his peers, because they can't discipline themselves to do so. This person will also attract the attention of the Willie Sutton types—the Internal Revenue Service—and they will take 30% of the earnings. The net effect is that he will earn 4% after taxes. Table (1) will show the results of this procedure. The C/D account now has an after-tax amount of $41,071.13. It is time to start the self-financing of car purchases from the system now. If this person is dull enough to let the car salesman know that he has over $40,000 in his C/D account the salesman will, most assuredly, say, "Son, you don't need to be looking at a Taurus—let me show you this BMW!" But this young man has done some studying and concludes that if he jumps through that hoop he will end up with the same results as Method C, except on a grand scale. So he *withdraws* $10,550 from the C/D account, takes it plus his trade-in car, and purchases the Taurus.

He continues to fund the monthly savings account and annually withdraws $3,030 from it to purchase a new C/D each year. He is playing "honest banker" with himself but he is *using someone else's bank to do it.* The *dividends* of the bank are going to the *stockholders of the bank*. He is earning only the *interest* that the bank is paying him. There are several "characters in the play" that must be considered.

- The Stockholder or owner of the bank— earns dividends.

- The C/D holder—earns interest.

- Administrators at the bank (hired help)— earn salaries.

- The borrower of money. *An absolute necessity in the whole scene.* Nothing happens without him. He pays for the whole works above.

Table (1) shows the results of this procedure over the same 44 years as compared with the previous three methods. Figure (1) is the graphical depiction of the data in Table (1). There is a significant difference between the results of Method C and Method D. It is the result of three additional years of accumulation *and* all seven years are at an additional amount ($5,000). He is taking the necessity of capitalization seriously.

METHOD E—The FIFTH method is using dividend-paying life insurance as a depositary of the necessary capital to create the banking system to finance the automobiles. This person puts the same $5,000 per year, as in the foregoing method, into very high-premium life insurance with a mutual life insurance company. Recall the diagram back on page 38. (There are some exceptions to this requirement. There are *some* stock companies that have dividend-paying policies). After the seven years of capitalization, this person *withdraws dividends in the amount required to pay cash for the car.* This process *does not* involve policy loans. In order to play *honest banker* with himself, he must make premium payments to the policy instead of to a finance company—but in the same amount that he would have to pay to one, in this case, $3,030 per year—the same as the person using Method D.

Notice that in Table (1) the results favor Method D up through year 14—but from that point on the difference favors Method E in an accelerating fashion. There is a very simple explanation for this effect. Hardly anyone takes into consideration that the Banker in Method D that issued the C/Ds went through a long and costly process of getting a Bank Charter and winning the deposits of customers (whose money he lends to borrowers). It is just like getting the grocery business started as described in the beginning of this book. Every time a person buys a life insurance policy he is *starting a business from scratch*. There is the inevitable delay in results in getting a business started. The life insurance company is nothing more than an *administrator* of the plan the policy owner purchased. If you have seen an Executive Vice-President at a Life Insurance Company and an Executive Vice-President at a Bank, they could change jobs every six months and no one would know the difference! For practical purposes they do the same thing. It is the *Stockholder* (or Bank Owner) that makes all the difference. This is the party that puts up all the capital to start the business and earns the rewards or suffers the loss.

Both methods, D & E, are all dependent on borrowers to make their business successful and the *market* sets the rate—not Alan Greenspan at the Federal Reserve Bank. In the Life Insurance method the policy owner is earning *both interest and dividends*. There are no stockholders! The cost of administration in both cases is a "wash." Look at year 51 in Table (1) and compare the difference between the two methods. The difference is what went to the *stockholders* at the bank in Method D, if it was accumulated on a tax-deferred basis for that period of time ($964,638 - $258,927 = $705,710). To make all this money the Banker had to go through that gory mess that was described on pages 19-20. But, hardly anyone takes this into consideration. They all tend to look at the early years of the two methods and conclude, "Life Insurance is a poor place to accumulate wealth." They couldn't be more wrong!

Continue studying Table (1) and you will realize that you are just now discovering the *real power* of the life insurance method—the comparison of the retirement income that can be realized from each method. Assuming a withdrawal of $50,000 per year from each, please notice that the C/D account is out of money in five years and eight months. But the life insurance policy is *still growing* although $50,000 is being withdrawn from dividends until the cost basis is recovered, and from policy loans from that point on, hence the income is not a taxable event. Assume that the insured dies at the 65th year (Age 85) she has withdrawn $650,000 on dividend income and then the net death benefit for her beneficiary is $1,365,057! If she lived longer then the income would continue and the death benefit would never get below $1,000,000. There is *no real comparison* between the methods.

This is the essence of what *The Infinite Banking Concept* is all about—recovering the interest that one normally pays to some banking institution and then lending it to others so that the policy owner makes what a banking institution does. It is like building an environment in the airplane world where you have a perpetual "tailwind" instead of a perpetual "headwind." Simple, isn't it? Controlling the environment is much more productive than trying to make the airplane fly 5 miles per hour faster!

Let's review the "Characters in the Play" once more--Shakespeare said, "All the world is a stage and all the people are actors thereon." Acknowledging this thought from him, I say, "When it comes to the subject of finance, frankly, most folks don't understand the play. Worse than that, they can't get the characters in the play straight!"

So, let's compare the activity and characters in a conventional bank and that of a life insurance contract with a mutual, dividend-paying company. A bank can't operate without "hired help." Neither can a life insurance company. A bank must lend money or it is not in business. So does a life insurance company. (These two items are a "wash".) The stockholder at the bank earns dividends. So does the life policy owner. The C/D holder at a bank earns interest. So does the life policy owner (guaranteed cash value).

The only difference in the two is how earnings are allocated. The life policy owner gets both interest (guaranteed cash value) AND dividends!

On page 45, there is a difference in values in the early years up through year 14, though the outlay and car purchases, along with repayments are the same.

That's because, when you buy a life policy, you are literally starting a new business from "scratch." There is a "start-up cost" in creating a new business. It takes a life company about 13 years to amortize the "cost of acquisition" of a new policy.

In order to issue a C/D a banker has to create a bank. From the start of the idea until it's "break even" point, it will take the average bank about 15 years. Practically no one seems to recognize this fact.

So, what is the banker's reward for all his efforts? Look at year 51 and compare the results of each method. Subtract the $258,927 from the $964,638 and you have isolated what went to the banker, if it has been compounded over that period of years. The death benefit is not a factor in this comparison. It is a bonus to the policy owner.

TABLE 1

Year	Deposits	Car payments to each respective system	Car purchases made by withdrawals from each respective system	Cash in CD account, METHOD D		Cash in IBC method, METHOD E	
1	$5,000.00			$5,200.00		$1,933.00	
2	$5,000.00			$10,608.00		$6,359.00	
3	$5,000.00			$16,232.32		$11,514.00	
4	$5,000.00			$22,081.61		$17,012.00	
5	$5,000.00			$28,164.88		$22,880.00	
6	$5,000.00			$34,491.47		$29,150.00	
7	$5,000.00			$41,071.13		$35,960.00	
8		$3,030.00	$10,550.00	$34,893.18		$29,898.00	
9		$3,030.00		$39,440.10		$34,778.00	
10		$3,030.00		$44,168.91		$40,076.00	
11		$3,030.00		$49,086.86		$45,821.00	
12		$3,030.00	$10,550.00	$43,229.53		$40,628.00	
13		$3,030.00		$48,109.92		$46,441.00	
14		$3,030.00		$53,185.51		$52,744.00	
15		$3,030.00		$58,464.13		$59,570.00	
16		$3,030.00	$10,550.00	$52,981.90		$55,619.00	
17		$3,030.00		$58,252.37		$62,832.00	
18		$3,030.00		$63,733.67		$70,727.00	
19		$3,030.00		$69,434.22		$79,342.00	
20		$3,030.00	$10,550.00	$64,390.78		$77,308.00	
21		$3,030.00		$70,117.62		$86,368.00	
22		$3,030.00		$76,073.52		$96,243.00	
23		$3,030.00		$82,267.66		$106,996.00	
24		$3,030.00	$10,550.00	$77,737.57		$107,287.00	
25		$3,030.00		$83,998.27		$119,085.00	
26		$3,030.00		$90,509.40		$131,930.00	
27		$3,030.00		$97,280.98		$145,910.00	
28		$3,030.00	$10,550.00	$93,351.42		$149,691.00	
29		$3,030.00		$100,236.67		$165,270.00	
30		$3,030.00		$107,397.34		$182,301.00	
31		$3,030.00		$114,844.43		$200,532.00	
32		$3,030.00	$10,550.00	$111,617.41		$208,931.00	
33		$3,030.00		$119,233.31		$229,431.00	
34		$3,030.00		$127,153.84		$251,603.00	
35		$3,030.00		$135,391.19		$275,565.00	
36		$3,030.00	$10,550.00	$132,986.04		$290,057.00	
37		$3,030.00		$141,456.68		$317,126.00	
38		$3,030.00		$150,266.15		$346,394.00	
39		$3,030.00		$159,428.00		$378,019.00	
40		$3,030.00	$10,550.00	$157,984.32		$400,751.00	
41		$3,030.00		$167,454.89		$436,716.00	
42		$3,030.00		$177,304.28		$475,589.00	
43		$3,030.00		$187,548.33		$517,593.00	
44		$3,030.00	$10,550.00	$187,228.76		$551,593.00	
45		$3,030.00		$197,869.11		$599,579.00	
46		$3,030.00		$208,935.07		$651,440.00	
47		$3,030.00		$220,443.67		$707,442.00	
48		$3,030.00	$10,550.00	$221,440.62		$756,415.00	
49	**Retirement**	$3,030.00		$233,449.45	**Retirement**	$820,680.00	
50	**Income**	$3,030.00		$245,938.62	**Income**	$889,940.00	
51		$3,030.00		$258,927.37		$964,638.00	
52	-$50,000.00			$217,284.46	-$50,000.00	$987,757.00	
53	-$50,000.00			$173,975.84	-$50,000.00	$996,804.00	
54	-$50,000.00			$128,934.88	-$50,000.00	$1,005,214.00	
55	-$50,000.00			$82,092.27	-$50,000.00	$1,013,691.00	
56	-$50,000.00			$33,375.96	-$50,000.00	$1,022,162.00	
57	-$33,375.96			$0.00	-$50,000.00	$1,030,442.00	
58					-$50,000.00	$1,038,573.00	
59					-$50,000.00	$1,046,485.00	
60					-$50,000.00	$1,054,126.00	
61					-$50,000.00	$1,061,423.00	**Death Benefit**
62					-$50,000.00	$1,068,310.00	
63					-$50,000.00	$1,074,496.00	
64					-$50,000.00	$1,080,094.00	$1,365,057.00
Totals	-$283,376.00	$168,320.00	$116,050.00		-$650,000.00		$1,365,057.00

WHOLE LIFE PAID-UP AT 96

POLICY YEAR	AGE-START OF YEAR	NET PRE-MIUM	ANNUAL LOAN	CUM LOAN	AFTER TAX LOAN INT	CUM NET A/T OUTLAY	NET CASH VALUE	NET DEATH BENEFIT
1	21	$5,000	$0	$0	$0	$5,000	$1,933	$477,973
2	22	$5,000	$0	$0	$0	$10,000	$6,359	$491,598
3	23	$5,000	$0	$0	$0	$15,000	$11,514	$506,382
4	24	$5,000	$0	$0	$0	$20,000	$17,012	$521,723
5	25	$5,000	$0	$0	$0	$25,000	$22,880	$537,646
6	26	$5,000	$0	$0	$0	$30,000	$29,150	$554,179
7	27	$5,000	$0	$0	$0	$35,000	$35,960	$571,481
8	28	-$7,520	$0	$0	$0	$27,480	$29,898	$516,580
9	29	$3,030	$0	$0	$0	$30,510	$34,778	$522,356
10	30	$3,030	$0	$0	$0	$33,540	$40,076	$529,236
11	31	$3,030	$0	$0	$0	$36,570	$45,821	$537,244
12	32	-$7,520	$0	$0	$0	$29,050	$40,628	$491,663
13	33	$3,030	$0	$0	$0	$32,080	$46,441	$499,337
14	34	$3,030	$0	$0	$0	$35,110	$52,744	$508,074
15	35	$3,030	$0	$0	$0	$38,140	$59,570	$517,962
16	36	-$7,520	$0	$0	$0	$30,620	$55,619	$481,106
17	37	$3,030	$0	$0	$0	$33,650	$62,832	$491,439
18	38	$3,030	$0	$0	$0	$36,680	$70,727	$503,252
19	39	$3,030	$0	$0	$0	$39,710	$79,342	$516,619
20	40	-$7,520	$0	$0	$0	$32,190	$77,308	$489,459
21	41	$3,030	$0	$0	$0	$35,220	$86,368	$503,971
22	42	$3,030	$0	$0	$0	$38,250	$96,243	$520,050
23	43	$3,030	$0	$0	$0	$41,280	$106,996	$537,727
24	44	-$7,520	$0	$0	$0	$33,760	$107,287	$519,857
25	45	$3,030	$0	$0	$0	$36,790	$119,085	$538,959
26	46	$3,030	$0	$0	$0	$39,820	$131,930	$559,692
27	47	$3,030	$0	$0	$0	$42,850	$145,910	$582,116
28	48	-$7,520	$0	$0	$0	$35,330	$149,691	$573,383
29	49	$3,030	$0	$0	$0	$38,360	$165,270	$597,728
30	50	$3,030	$0	$0	$0	$41,390	$182,201	$623,911
31	51	$3,030	$0	$0	$0	$44,420	$200,532	$651,941
32	52	-$7,520	$0	$0	$0	$36,900	$208,931	$652,539
33	53	$3,030	$0	$0	$0	$39,930	$229,461	$682,786
34	54	$3,030	$0	$0	$0	$42,960	$251,603	$714,971
35	55	$3,030	$0	$0	$0	$45,990	$275,565	$749,184
36	56	-$7,520	$0	$0	$0	$38,470	$290,057	$759,404
37	57	$3,030	$0	$0	$0	$41,500	$317,126	$796,501
38	58	$3,030	$0	$0	$0	$44,530	$346,394	$835,725
39	59	$3,030	$0	$0	$0	$47,560	$378,019	$877,142
40	60	-$7,520	$0	$0	$0	$40,040	$400,751	$897,507
41	61	$3,030	$0	$0	$0	$43,070	$436,716	$942,417
42	62	$3,030	$0	$0	$0	$46,100	$475,589	$989,987

POLICY YEAR	AGE-START OF YEAR	NET PRE-MIUM	ANNUAL LOAN	CUM LOAN	AFTER TAX LOAN INT	CUM NET A/T OUTLAY	NET CASH VALUE	NET DEATH BENEFIT
43	63	$3,030	$0	$0	$0	$49,130	$517,593	$1,040,522
44	64	-$7,520	$0	$0	$0	$41,610	$551,559	$1,073,410
45	65	$3,030	$0	$0	$0	$44,640	$599,579	$1,129,528
46	66	$3,030	$0	$0	$0	$47,670	$651,440	$1,189,216
47	67	$3,030	$0	$0	$0	$50,700	$707,442	$1,252,664
48	68	-$7,520	$0	$0	$0	$43,180	$756,415	$1,301,012
49	69	$3,030	$0	$0	$0	$46,210	$820,680	$1,371,164
50	70	$3,030	$0	$0	$0	$49,240	$889,940	$1,445,334
51	71	$3,030	$0	$0	$0	$52,270	$964,628	$1,523,993	← ③
52	72	-$50,000	$0	$0	$0	$2,270	$987,757	$1,521,472
53	73	-$50,000	$15,035	$15,035	$716	-$47,730	$996,804	$1,505,909
54	74	-$50,000	$16,502	$31,537	$1,502	-$97,730	$1,005,214	$1,490,592
55	75	-$50,000	$17,327	$48,864	$2,327	-$147,730	$1,013,691	$1,476,202
56	76	-$50,000	$18,193	$67,057	$3,193	-$197,730	$1,022,162	$1,462,666
57	77	-$50,000	$19,103	$86,160	$4,103	-$247,730	$1,030,442	$1,449,661
58	78	-$50,000	$20,058	$106,218	$5,058	-$297,730	$1,038,573	$1,437,012
59	79	-$50,000	$21,061	$127,278	$6,061	-$347,730	$1,046,485	$1,424,597
60	80	-$50,000	$22,114	$149,392	$7,114	-$397,730	$1,054,126	$1,412,326
61	81	-$50,000	$23,220	$172,612	$8,220	-$447,730	$1,061,423	$1,400,218
62	82	-$50,000	$24,381	$196,993	$9,381	-$497,730	$1,068,310	$1,388,355
63	83	-$50,000	$25,600	$222,592	$10,600	-$547,730	$1,074,496	$1,376,591
64	84	-$50,000	$26,880	$249,472	$11,880	-$597,730	$1,080,094	$1,365,057
65	85	-$50,000	$28,224	$277,695	$13,224	-$647,730	$1,084,995	$1,353,680	← ④
66	86	-$50,000	$29,635	$307,330	$14,635	-$697,730	$1,088,911	$1,342,049
67	87	-$50,000	$31,117	$338,447	$16,117	-$747,730	$1,091,696	$1,329,863
68	88	-$50,000	$32,672	$371,119	$17,672	-$797,730	$1,093,310	$1,316,851
69	89	-$50,000	$34,306	$405,425	$19,306	-$847,730	$1,093,636	$1,302,676
70	90	-$50,000	$36,021	$441,446	$21,021	-$897,730	$1,092,623	$1,286,999
71	91	-$50,000	$37,822	$479,269	$22,822	-$947,730	$1,090,515	$1,269,713
72	92	-$50,000	$39,713	$518,982	$24,713	-$997,730	$1,087,129	$1,250,200
73	93	-$50,000	$41,699	$560,681	$26,699	-$1,147,730	$1,082,570	$1,227,983
74	94	-$50,000	$43,784	$604,465	$28,784	-$1,097,730	$1,077,044	$1,202,635
75	95	-$50,000	$45,973	$650,438	$30,973	-$1,147,730	$1,070,680	$1,173,790

FEMALE, AGE 21, Dividends to Paid-Up Additions $464,147 L/96
PREFERRED NON-SMOKER Premium $3,030
Paid-Up Additions Rider $1,970
Total Premium $5,000

① $5,000 per year for seven years is the "capitalization phase."

② -$7,520 is "short-hand" for a withdrawal of dividends to finance a $10,550 car purchase, and a premium payment of $3,030 in lieu of an identical payment to a finance company. This is done each four years.

③ At year 51 there is a death benefit of $1,523,993—which has a cash value of $964,638. She can begin a withdrawal of dividends of $50,000 per year for life.

④ Assuming death at age 85, she has drawn out $647,730 plus the cumulative outlay of $52,270—and still delivers $1,353,680 to her beneficiary.

⑤ If she lives longer, the $50,000 per year income will never run out.

EXPANDING THE SYSTEM TO ACCOMMODATE ALL INCOME

It always sounds a bit strange to people when I say, "premiums and income should match." Let's start with a very basic fact—doesn't *all your money* go through someone else's bank now? When you get your paycheck, what do you do with it? Right! You deposit it in *someone else's bank*. Then you write checks against it to buy the things you want in life. While it is in the bank, the banker lends your money to someone else and makes a good living doing it!

It seems a little ridiculous, but my All-American man on page 17 is depositing *all* of his paycheck in a bank—and then writing checks for 34.5% of every dollar to *pay interest alone* back to someone else's banking system. He will never see that money again! It is gone forever. Why does he behave this way? Because no one has ever explained to him a better way of doing things! Once a pattern of life is learned in a culture it is nigh unto impossible to change. His paradigm is *fixed*! Set in concrete! The peer pressure and conventional wisdom is overwhelming. But, that doesn't mean that it can't be done. When he builds a banking system through life insurance, makes loans to himself to buy automobiles—and pays back to the policy (or policies) the same payment he would have to pay a banking institution—then he makes what the banking institution would have made off of him. And it is all done on a tax-deferred basis! The interest he pays *never* leaves his account and control. If this is done consistently throughout life it will make a tremendous difference in his financial picture.

So far, we have only looked at what will happen if we create a system that will finance just one automobile every four years. Why not expand the system by starting another policy that will finance the other automobile in the family? This will, of course, require the capitalization period of seven years at the rate of $5,000 per year, but at the end of that time we have kissed the automobile financing business good-bye forever!

In time, the total cash values in all policies are adequate enough to take the next step—self-insuring the automobiles for comprehensive and collision coverage. Please note that I did not say *liability coverage*—that is the insurance that covers you in the event of a law suit against you. Comprehensive and collision coverage is for damage done to your car in an accident. This is required coverage if you have the car financed with some other banking service, but if you are using your own banking system it is your decision to make.

Why not do it through life insurance policies? After all, what did the automobile insurance companies do to get into their business? First, they got actuarial data to determine the probabilities of a car accident and its attendant costs that are peculiar to the make and model of car. Then they got rate-makers to determine how much should be charged for the coverage. Next, they turned it all over to attorneys that made legal and binding contracts out of the foregoing information. Lastly, they had insurance agents call on you to see if you would like to insure your car with their company. (Does all this sound familiar? Go back to page 21 and review the steps in creating life insurance.)

The auto insurance company has to put the premiums to work *in the same places as the life insurance company!* They also have to pay claims and administrative costs, just like a life insurance company. And they also pay *dividends*—to whoever owns the company—just like a life insurance company. Can you see that, once you get a substantial base of cash values in life insurance, you have all the elements of an automobile insurance company, except pricing of the product? All you have to do to self-insure is to find out how much more you should put into life policies to assume that risk. That is a simple matter—just get a quote from some prominent auto insurer on your make and model of car. If the quote is $750 per year for $500 deductible, don't pay your life policies that amount—pay them $1,000 for *zero deductible!* If you had an accident, you were going to have to pay the $500 deductible first, anyway.

Next is the matter of the house mortgage. When enough money is accumulated in cash values in the foregoing policies to pay off the mortgage, then borrow from them and do so, *making sure that you pay the policies whatever would have to be paid to a mortgage company to amortize such indebtedness.* Of course, you can speed up this ability by adding new life insurance on someone (it doesn't matter who the insured is—all you want to do is *own* the policy so that you can control the cash values). This repayment of the policies should also include "closing costs" that would be associated with the refinancing of a house mortgage. Remember to *play the game*— whatever the next-door neighbor would have to do to refinance his house with a new mortgage, you do to yourself at your own banking system. The money will go to *your policies* being managed by the life insurance company.

REVIEW - PART III

Note that a car could be financed at the end of the fourth year in both methods.

Q — What happens if a car is financed at that time *and the system continues to be capitalized* for the total of seven years?

A — Both accounts would result in better performance than depicted but E would result in a greater increase than D.

Q — Why?

A — Because E is earning *both dividends and interest*. Both methods involve administrators (which negates that function as a factor in the results). The *market* determines the rate at which money can be lent. A bank cannot lend money at a significantly higher rate than a life insurance company, nor vice versa.

Note that a $21,100 car financing package could be handled at the end of year seven in both methods.

Q — If so, what should the payments be?

A — $6,060 ($520/month).

Q — What would happen to the results in both cases?

A — They would increase even more, but E would be better than D.

Q — What if the person in both cases decides to pay $7,000 on the above case?

A — The "extra payment" goes straight to the "bottom line" of the respective methods.

Method D has better net figures during the seven years of capitalization.

Q — Why?

A — Because, in method D, the fact that the bank went through a *long and costly* process of getting established has been left out of the scenario. In method E the policy-owner is *starting up a new business that never existed before.* There is always a cost of starting up a conventional bank. The life insurance company is simply, in effect, an *administrator* of the plan (policy). Earnings (dividends) and interest both go to the policy-owner.

I have told you this so that my joy may be in you and that your joy may be complete.
- John 15:11

PART IV - EQUIPMENT FINANCING

Now that we have established the fact that a dividend-paying life insurance policy has all the characteristics of a banking system, let's refresh your memory of the steps it takes to get into the banking business and then use the system to enhance the things that you are already doing within your regular line of business.

All you have to do is select an appropriate plan of life insurance with a quality "dividend-paying life insurance company (you need to have good administrative "hired help") and put some money into it. You must build the "capitalization phase" over a period of time, such as four years minimum. You may find it necessary to accumulate the capital over a longer period of time. Indeed, additional capital makes the system more profitable. Whoever heard of a grocer complaining about having to fill the shelves on *five* gondolas in his store instead of *four?* He knows full well that the additional merchandise (capital) will improve his profitability. Neither should someone complain about additional capital (premiums) paid into a life insurance policy.

There are no licenses required and no customers to seek out. No accounting. No engineering. It has all been done beforehand by the life insurance company—your "hired help." You surely don't get those advantages when starting up any other business!

Suppose that this 30 year old man, who is in the logging business, adopts such a plan and puts $40,000 of capital per year into his "banking system" for four years. The policy he is using is a "Life Paid-Up at age 65" with a premium of $15,000 per year and a Paid-Up Insurance Rider premium in the amount of $25,000. (See illustration #1.) Notice that at the end of the first four years the total cash value ($157,363) and his cumulative outlay ($160,000) are practically identical.

Beginning the fifth year, no further premiums are required because the current dividend ($6,339),

plus surrender of some of the paid-up insurance will pay the base premium ($15,000) from that point on. Notice the death benefit at the end of the fourth year ($1,684,787), and compare it with the end of the fifth year ($1,651,077). The difference between the numbers is the amount of paid-up insurance surrendered to pay the annual $15,000 premium—resulting in no "out of pocket" outlay. His administrators, the life insurance company, lend the money out to various places and, after expenses of operation and paying out an occasional death claim, show that he has something like $1,517,320 in cash value 36 years later, which has a death benefit of $2,406,948 at that time. The death benefit has grown, over the years, because all dividends in excess of the annual premium are used to buy additional paid-up insurance. This increase is all done on a tax-free accumulation basis. Taxation does not occur until the amount withdrawn exceeds the premiums paid into the policy.

The insured is now age 66 and is considering retirement. He can begin to withdraw $92,000 per year in dividends to meet that need from that point on—no matter how long he lives! Suppose he dies at age 85. At that point he has recovered all the premiums he has paid into the policy ($160,000), plus $1,588,000—and he *still* delivers $2,407,736 in death benefit to his beneficiary.

He could decide to draw a larger income from dividend credits—but doing so would diminish the capital base and the ultimate death benefit. Conversely, he could decide to draw a smaller income from dividends, in which case, the capital base would increase and so would the residual death benefit. Under the scenario depicted thus far, the income will become *income-taxable* when the amount of income received exceeds his cost basis (premiums paid in— in this case $160,000). There is no need to dwell on this matter at length at this point, as you will see by the next series of examples.

No matter how you look at it, the above is a pretty good scenario. But, then it dawns on the young man –"I'm paying $16,000 *per month* to that pool of money for the equipment used in my logging business. The finance company (gate-keeper & toll-taker) is borrowing the money they lend me from life insurance companies, adding a surcharge to it, and retailing it to me! (See Figure 2 and Exhibit 1). Why, that's the equivalent of my wife shopping for groceries at Winn-Dixie when we already own a grocery store!" So he asks his life insurance agent, "Can I finance a logging truck from my cash values?" Of course he can! He outranks all possible borrowers in access to the pool of money that *must be lent* to make the life insurance plan work.

Exhibit 1 is an exact copy of a financing package on a new Peterbilt truck from a well-known finance company that buys "blocks of money" from life insurance companies, adds an up-charge to it and retails it to people outside the gate in the "Great Wall of China." This event occurred in 1984. He paid $65,790 for the truck, with $13,190 down payment and financed $52,600 for four years. To amortize the indebtedness requires a monthly payment of $1,502 per month (item 10). Nowhere on the page is there any indication of an interest rate charged—it isn't required—since this is a "commercial loan." But, it can be easily calculated—it is slightly above 15% annual percentage rate. At the end of four years he has paid out $72,096 (item 8). He financed $52,600, so a little "third grade arithmetic" reveals that he paid $19,496 in interest (item 7) over the period.

Divide the interest paid out by the total payments and it will tell you *what part* of each payment is interest. It is 27 cents! Every time he pays out $1.00—twenty seven cents is interest—*if he pays off the entire indebtedness* over four years. If he trades-in the truck in two years then the ratio is much higher. He is making a "so-so" living in logging and the "Banking business" is living well off him!

So, what happens at the end of four years? Clue: the odometer on the truck reads something like 400,000 miles! He is back at the Peterbilt place, trading in his old truck on a new one. This time, the dealer may allow him a trade-in value of something like $18,000. But, the price of the new truck has gone up, too, and he keeps financing about $52,600 on every truck that he buys. That has been going on for years. His accountant tells him, "Look at how you are *building equity* in your equipment!" That's true—but he is building equity in the wrong place. He should be building equity in the *banking business that finances his trucks!* Everyone should be in two businesses— the one in which you make your living and the

other should be the banking business that *finances* whatever you do for a living. Of the two businesses, banking is the most important. Businesses come and go—but banking is eternal. Just think about it for a moment—the richest man in the U.S. today is Bill Gates. The business did not exist 25 years ago.

When he buys the truck this time he doesn't use the finance company. He calls his "gopher" at the insurance company and asks, "Can I borrow $52,600 from my policy to finance a new truck?" Look at line 4, column 6, in the next illustration (2) and you see the cash value is $157,363, just like it was in the previous example. This is the amount of money that the life insurance company *must lend to someone* in order to make the plan of insurance work. Of course he can borrow $52,600.

Pay close attention to this point—*it is vital that you understand that he must set up a loan repayment plan that equals or exceeds what he would have had to pay the finance company that he was using in the past.* His life insurance agent should coach him at this point that "The policy loan interest rate is 8% — but, we are not going to play that game. We are going to call the finance company you *were* using and ask them what you would have to pay if you financed it with them. That is what you are going to have to pay." Of course, the policy-owner can tell him to "get lost—I'm not going to pay *any interest at all*. It *is my money!"* Or, maybe, he says, "I'm only going to pay 3.9%, just like you see on the TV commercials."

In either of the foregoing responses the life insurance agent needs to take him back to the grocery store story on page 15 and explain it to him *one more time*. If he still does not understand it, he needs to take him back to the First National Bank of Midland, TX story on page 19 and go through it *one more time, also*. If he still does not understand why he should pay retail market rates, then the agent needs to resign his relationship with him, draw a line through his name and forget him. He is either un-teachable— or he is a thief! Neither makes a good business associate. But, if the agent is *really good* at his job, he will convince him to pay $1,600 per month! The extra cash flow becomes capital in the system and enables his "gophers" at the life insurance company to lend more money to all those other borrowers. This extra money *does not go to the general portfolio of the company*—it goes to *his policy* that is being administered by the company on his behalf.

So, examine illustration #2 closely. Note the year 5, column 1 and you see (-) $34,600 expressed as an outlay. That is "shorthand" for the fact that he borrowed $52,600 that year and paid back $18,000 ($1,500 per month). Notice that the debt is being reduced to zero at the end of four years. Remember that the policy loan provision calls for interest at 8% — but he is repaying his policy at the rate of a bit over 15%. It should be obvious that he will repay the loan before the four years are up. The additional $1,500 per month becomes additional premiums and adds to the capital base.

Go to line 36 (his age 65) and look at the cash value now in comparison with the previous illustration. Note that the cash value is now $1,988,254 compared with $1,517,320. He made $470,934 by financing just one truck with his bank! The "gophers" at the life insurance company had nothing to do with this phenomenon. It was all on account of what the policy-owner did. Note that the retirement income has gone up to $125,000 per year. Again, assuming death at age 85, he has recovered his capital input plus $2,034,800 and still delivered $3,119,289 to his beneficiary.

The policy-owner says, "That's amazing! Can I finance *two trucks* through "my bank?" Assuming the same $52,600 financing package on each (total $105,200), of course he can. Look at illustration #3. Again, there is $157,363 available for loan at the end of the first four years. In this case he must repay $36,000 per year in order to be an "honest banker" with himself. Now, look at line 36, column 6, and you see $2,459,578 in cash value. He has picked up an additional $471,324 by shopping at home for his truck financing. In addition, the retirement income from dividends has gone up to $150,000 per year and the death benefit at age 85 becomes $3,992,624.

He is even more amazed, and asks, "Can I finance *three trucks* through this system?" In this case, he is *trying to do too much financing with too little capital*. He would be much wiser to establish a "branch office" to his banking system by capitalizing another policy. Nevertheless, it is theoretically possible to do so with this one.

Look at illustration #4. Notice the end result at line 36, column 6—there is $2,928,933 in cash value. The dividend income at retirement time is up to $175,000 per year, resulting in recovering his capital input, plus $2,675,959 in total income by age 85—and still delivers $5,085,598 to his beneficiary.

Remember, the wisest thing he could do is *add additional policies* to his banking system as early as possible to enhance his ability to finance his *entire inventory* of equipment. But, he can *still* improve on the results of the last example. Look at illustration #5. It is the same as the previous one until line 13. At this point he can finance all four of his logging trucks plus one of the logging tractors. (Logging tractors cost *twice* as much as trucks. And the Tree-shear costs *even more* than that). Now note the cash value at his age 65 is $3,518,411. Compare this with the cash value in illustration #1, where the company "gophers" did all the lending to other borrowers ($1,517,320) and you see that "shopping at home" resulted in over $2,000,000 in additional value.

Also, note the yearly dividend in column 5, line 36 in illustration #1 ($71,942). Now, compare it with the same point in illustration #4 ($140,279). The life insurance company's dividend scale *did not change*! They had nothing to do with this improvement. It was all on account of what the policy-owner did. The "gophers" at the life insurance company made just as much money in the first illustration as they did in the last illustration. In fact, the "gophers" cannot make a profit. They earn salaries, and can earn bonuses, if their efforts are superior—but only the policy owners can "make money" through improved dividends. The difference in results goes to his policy—not the general portfolio of the company.

At this point, consideration should be given to how to improve the results even further. Look at illustration #5, and note the cash value at the end of the second year. Question: Can a truck be financed at that point? Yes! But, remember, he should continue to capitalize the policy for a total of four years. But, anytime he can cut the "blood-suckers" out of the pattern and have that same financial energy flow through his banking system, he should do so. It should be obvious that this will improve all the cash value results below that point. If it isn't, then go back and read this chapter over and over until it dawns. If it still doesn't register, then go back and review the grocery store story and the First National Bank story. If this doesn't do the job, then I don't know if I can be of help.

Another improvement can be achieved by

EQUIPMENT FINANCING ILLUSTRATION 1

START YR	AGE	NET ANN OUTLAY	ANNUAL LOAN	GROSS INTEREST	CUMULATIVE LOAN	TOTAL DIVIDEND	NET CASH VALUE YR END	CUM NET OUTLAY	DEATH BENEFIT
1	30	$40,000	$0	$0	$0	$0	$24,029	$40,000	$1,342,420
2	31	$40,000	$0	$0	$0	$0	$65,282	$80,000	$1,448,237
3	32	$40,000	$0	$0	$0	$2,821	$109,637	$120,000	$1,565,319
4	33	$40,000	$0	$0	$0	$4,494	$157,363	$160,000	$1,684,787
5	34	$0	$0	$0	$0	$6,339	$167,182	$160,000	$1,651,077
6	35	$0	$0	$0	$0	$6,359	$177,803	$160,000	$1,617,227
7	36	$0	$0	$0	$0	$6,827	$189,303	$160,000	$1,586,373
8	37	$0	$0	$0	$0	$7,393	$201,772	$160,000	$1,558,701
9	38	$0	$0	$0	$0	$8,032	$215,294	$160,000	$1,534,303
10	39	$0	$0	$0	$0	$8,735	$229,940	$160,000	$1,513,222
11	40	$0	$0	$0	$0	$9,500	$245,790	$160,000	$1,495,466
12	41	$0	$0	$0	$0	$10,325	$262,987	$160,000	$1,481,114
13	42	$0	$0	$0	$0	$11,273	$281,585	$160,000	$1,470,253
14	43	$0	$0	$0	$0	$12,233	$301,720	$160,000	$1,462,786
15	44	$0	$0	$0	$0	$13,296	$323,507	$160,000	$1,458,790
16	45	$0	$0	$0	$0	$14,409	$347,078	$160,000	$1,458,250
17	46	$0	$0	$0	$0	$15,634	$372,555	$160,000	$1,461,233
18	47	$0	$0	$0	$0	$16,910	$400,109	$160,000	$1,467,729
19	48	$0	$0	$0	$0	$18,311	$429,894	$160,000	$1,477,823
20	49	$0	$0	$0	$0	$19,792	$462,092	$160,000	$1,491,562
21	50	$0	$0	$0	$0	$21,417	$496,851	$160,000	$1,510,003
22	51	$0	$0	$0	$0	$24,093	$534,403	$160,000	$1,533,598
23	52	$0	$0	$0	$0	$26,019	$575,015	$160,000	$1,561,290
24	53	$0	$0	$0	$0	$28,159	$618,942	$160,000	$1,593,313
25	54	$0	$0	$0	$0	$30,523	$666,427	$160,000	$1,629,892
26	55	$0	$0	$0	$0	$33,096	$717,776	$160,000	$1,671,237
27	56	$0	$0	$0	$0	$35,871	$773,220	$160,000	$1,717,463
28	57	$0	$0	$0	$0	$38,806	$833,139	$160,000	$1,768,699
29	58	$0	$0	$0	$0	$41,992	$897,818	$160,000	$1,825,120
30	59	$0	$0	$0	$0	$45,331	$967,607	$160,000	$1,886,785
31	60	$0	$0	$0	$0	$48,898	$1,042,969	$160,000	$1,953,959
32	61	$0	$0	$0	$0	$52,841	$1,124,212	$160,000	$2,026,980
33	62	$0	$0	$0	$0	$56,994	$1,211,884	$160,000	$2,106,079
34	63	$0	$0	$0	$0	$61,623	$1,306,418	$160,000	$2,191,756
35	64	$0	$0	$0	$0	$66,577	$1,408,285	$160,000	$2,284,301
36	65	$0	$0	$0	$0	$71,942	$1,517,320	$160,000	$2,406,948
37	66	-$92,000	$0	$0	$0	$76,620	$1,535,083	$68,000	$2,388,186
38	67	-$92,000	$0	$0	$0	$77,785	$1,553,719	-$24,000	$2,366,852
39	68	-$92,000	$0	$0	$0	$79,063	$1,573,317	-$116,000	$2,348,032
40	69	-$92,000	$0	$0	$0	$80,346	$1,593,760	-$208,000	$2,331,513
41	70	-$92,000	$0	$0	$0	$81,504	$1,615,244	-$300,000	$2,317,164
42	71	-$92,000	$0	$0	$0	$82,915	$1,637,846	-$392,000	$2,305,388
43	72	-$92,000	$0	$0	$0	$84,504	$1,661,661	-$484,000	$2,296,355
44	73	-$92,000	$0	$0	$0	$86,348	$1,686,737	-$576,000	$2,290,342
45	74	-$92,000	$0	$0	$0	$88,419	$1,713,164	-$668,000	$2,287,491
46	75	-$92,000	$0	$0	$0	$90,626	$1,740,933	-$760,000	$2,287,799
47	76	-$92,000	$0	$0	$0	$92,892	$1,769,997	-$852,000	$2,291,093
48	77	-$92,000	$0	$0	$0	$95,007	$1,800,385	-$944,000	$2,297,030
49	78	-$92,000	$0	$0	$0	$97,032	$1,832,206	-$1,036,000	$2,305,422
50	79	-$92,000	$0	$0	$0	$98,942	$1,865,492	-$1,128,000	$2,316,087
51	80	-$92,000	$0	$0	$0	$100,818	$1,900,340	-$1,220,000	$2,329,013
52	81	-$92,000	$0	$0	$0	$102,769	$1,936,871	-$1,312,000	$2,344,345
53	82	-$92,000	$0	$0	$0	$104,913	$1,975,174	-$1,404,000	$2,362,370
54	83	-$92,000	$0	$0	$0	$107,355	$2,015,361	-$1,496,000	$2,383,436
55	84	-$92,000	$0	$0	$0	$110,096	$2,057,446	-$1,588,000	$2,407,736

FIGURE 2

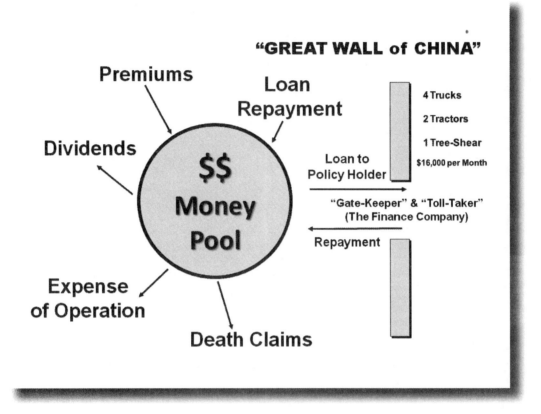

Whenever a large pool of cash is accumulated, there is always a barrier of some kind to keep most folks out. Hence my explanation of "The Great Wall of China."

And there is always some other party that has privileged access to that same pool. This is the "Gate-keeper & Toll-taker."

Our Logging contractor is borrowing money to finance his equipment from the "Gate-keeper & Toll-taker' (The Finance Company)—money that the finance company (FC) borrowed, in large quantities, from the life insurance company. The FC adds an up-charge to it and retails it to the logger. The logger pays the FC $16,000 per month and the FC repays the life insurance company a lower rate. The FC lives well off the flow of cash through his hands! It is this financial energy that can be captured by the policy-owner and accrue to his benefit—all on an income tax-free basis.

The policy-owner outranks all other possible borrowers from the life insurance pool of cash values that *must* be lent to someone in order for the plan to work.

EXHIBIT 1

DESCRIPTION OF VEHICLE - COLLATERAL (for security purposes only)

Year	Make-Model	Serial Number	New or Used	Price of Vehicle
1984	Peterbilt	LXP9DF9XDEN164673	New	$65,790.00

Buyer hereby grants a security interest in the above Vehicle and any additional collateral (collectively the "Collateral"), and any Additions and Accessions (as defined on the reverse side), to seller and its assigns to secure prompt payment of the indebtedness herein and performance of buyer's other obligations, including any additional indebtedness incurred as provided by this Contract and any extensions and renewals of the obligations and future advances. The security interest extends to the proceeds of the Collateral and the proceeds of any insurance policy.

Buyer also acknowledges that Seller has offered to sell the Vehicle for the cash Price indicated, but that buyer has chosen to purchase on the terms and conditions of this Contract:

1. TOTAL CASH PRICE (including: Sales Tax $ NA   :Title Fee $ NA   ) $ 65,790.00   (1)

2- TOTAL DOWN PAYMENT (consisting of Net Trade-in $ NA   : Cash $13,190.00 $13,190.00   (2)
   Description of Trade-in:

$ NA

Year	Make	Model	Serial No.	Trade-in Allowances

Payoff due to: Amount Due $ NA

3. UNPAID CASH PRICE (subtract 2 from 1) $52,600.00   (3)

4. INSURANCE

A. Required physical damage insurance

Physical damage insurance is required by this contract until the indebtedness is fully paid. Buyer has the option of furnishing such insurance either through existing policies owned or controlled by him or procuring or furnishing equivalent coverage through any insurance company authorized to do business in this state, provided, however, that with respect to dual interest insurance, Seller shall have the right to reject for reasonable cause any insurer offered by Buyer.

Insurance Company: Term   NA   months
(if applicable) Physical damage insurance not financed in-this contract.

$ NA   Deductible Collision   Premium $ NA   (4A)
$ NA   Deductible Comprehensive   Premium $ NA   (4A)
Other   Premium $ NA   (4A)

B. OPTIONAL Credit Insurance for the Term of this Contract.

Credit Life and Credit Accident and Health Insurance are not required by Seller, are not a factor in approval of the credit, and are included only 9 Buyer signs below.

I Do ___ I Do Not ____ Desire Credit Life insurance   Premium $ NA   (4B)
I Do ___ I Do Not ___ Desire Credit Accident and Health insurance   Premium $ NA   (4B)
Insurance Company

Buyer acknowledges disclosure of Credit Insurance charge above and requests and authorizes Seller to obtain insurance coverage checked and include the cost thereafter in item 4.

Buyer: Date:

Aggregate Amount of insurance (Add 4A and 4B) $ NA   (4)

5. OFFICIAL FEES (itemize)$ NA $ NA   (5)

6. PRINCIPAL BALANCE (Basic Time Price) (Add 3,4 and 5) $52.600.00   (6)

7. TIME PRICE DIFFERENTIAL (Finance Charge) $19,496.00   (7)

8. TIME BALANCE (Contract Balance) (Add 6 and 7) $72,096.00   (8)

9. TOTAL TIME SALE PRICE (Add 1,4,5, and 7) $85,286.00   (9)

10. PAYMENT SCHEDULE: The Time Balance (item 8) is payable to Seller or his assignee in __48__ installment(s) of $1,502.00 each, commencing December 19 8 4   followed by   installments of $ NA   each, commencing   19   followed by installments of $ NA   each, commencing 19   and on the   same day of each successive month thereafter, or as indicated below (if applicable) This Contract is not payable in installments of equal amounts.

An installment of $ NA   will be due on   . This will be a Balloon Payment (a payment more than twice the size of a regular installment). Larger installments will be due as follows:

11. DEFAULT CHARGE IN EVENT OF LATE PAYMENT. If any installment is not paid within 10 days after it is due, Buyer agrees to pay late charge equal to 5% of the unpaid installment not to exceed $5, or in lieu thereof, if allowed by law of the state in which this Contract is entered into, interest at the highest rate allowed, whichever is greater. Buyer represents and warrants that...

"back-dating the policy" for six months. Most all companies allow this. Pay the initial annual premium now, but ask the company for a policy date six months ago. This way it will be only eighteen months before being able to use the policy to cut the finance company out of the pattern. The earlier you are able to do so, the better the results.

This next improvement can be a big one. Go back to Exhibit 1, the finance company page. Note that Item 4, INSURANCE, takes up about one-third of the page. If they are going to finance your truck, they require you to insure it for comprehensive and collision coverage. That protects them against loss or damage to the equipment on which they have a lien. Liability insurance is another matter. It protects you against a possible law suit due to what your equipment may do to someone else or their property. The finance company does not require this—it is just good business to do so. But, guess which coverage has the biggest premium. Right! Comprehensive and collision. Typically, it runs about 75% of a "fully insured" premium.

Notice further, that all the blanks in Item 4 have NA (not applicable) inserted. That's because the finance company cannot force him to do insurance business with them—although they would like for him to do so *and finance that premium, too*! In this case, he used his own property and casualty insurance agent. His premium was $2,100 per year per truck, for $1,000 deductible.

I ask you; just what did the property and casualty insurance company have to do to create their company? They got a large amount of capital together, got actuaries to create tables of probabilities of an accident in a logging truck—got rate makers to figure how much they have to charge for each plan—got lawyers to make legal and binding contracts for them—and lastly, they got "clowns" to call on the logger and asked him if he wanted to buy logging truck insurance coverage. He responds, "I've got to—the finance company requires me to do so. I might as well do so with you." He puts $2,100 per year into the plan, the insurance company puts it to work in the same sort of places that a life insurance company does (*except they don't lend it to him*!). They also have to pay claims, and overhead cost — and at the end of the year they pay dividends to whoever put up the capital. (Look at page 21 and 22 and see if this doesn't all sound familiar). Do you realize that,

once he has a sizeable pool of capital in the form of cash values, he has all the elements of a property & casualty company—*except pricing*.

With that background, go to illustration #5, net cash value column, line 12. At this point he has $365,675 in readily available cash value. At this point he can consider *self-insuring* for comprehensive and collision coverage. (I did not say *liability* coverage!) But, he should pay his life insurance system of policies at least the same thing he was paying to the casualty company. In this case, it should not be $2,100 per year per truck for $1,000 deductible—it should be $2,500 per year per truck for *zero deductible!* Hopefully, I won't have to "draw little pictures" for this reasoning to be understood. Now he is making what the finance company was making off him *plus* what the casualty insurance company was making— *and it is all done on a tax-free accumulation basis.* Hopefully, you realize that, the figures in illustration #5 will be vastly improved when we have made all these refinements on introducing capital that was being bled off by other characters in the play. There is no way that the actual results of his system of life insurance policies will turn out like those depicted. If he obeys the above principles and practices them diligently, then the actual results should be significantly better than those depicted.

At this point, we turn to the matter of ownership of the policy (or policies). The company, a corporation, should not own it. He can improve the wealth building effects of the whole scenario by owning the policy himself, purchase the trucks himself, and *lease the trucks to the corporation*, making sure that he has charged a lease payment that is as high as possible. He can get that figure from some leasing company that leases similar equipment. By doing it this way he can have an interest deduction for the policy loans used to purchase the equipment (the loans are for business purpose)—he can depreciate the trucks over a reasonable time—and he has a "captive customer" to lease the equipment to that is sure to make the lease payments.

Finally, take a look at illustration #1, line 37 and note the stream of retirement income — $92,000 per year. This income stream becomes income-taxable when it exceeds the cost basis, which is $160,000 (see line 36, column 7). Now, go to illustration #5 and look at the stream of income ($225,000 per year). It, too becomes taxable when it exceeds the cost basis—

but look at the cost basis (line 36, column 7) and you see that it is now $946,184. The difference between this number and the original $160,000 of capital is the "interest"[1] he paid his policy during the entire period—and he gets it all back on a tax-free basis!!

All interest involved in these illustrations has been paid by *withdrawal* of additional dividend credits.

There can be even further improvements in the performance of the system. Just consider, at his age 66 he might sell all his equipment to someone just starting out in the logging business and make a deal with him to finance all his future needs for equipment when he has to replace each item. After all, he has over $3,500,000 that is readily available to do so. In fact, he can make a very good living during retirement just leasing equipment to any number of businesses. Try this for an exercise. Next time you are making a fairly long trip on the Interstate Highway system, keep a tally of the trucks you see and note the percentage that are leased. It will stagger your imagination. Have fun!

EQUIPMENT FINANCING ILLUSTRATIONS 1 - 6:

MALE, Age 30, Dividends to Paid-Up Additions
$1,233,439 L/65

Preferred Non-Smoker	$14,999.99
Paid-Up Additions Rider	$25,000.00
Total Premium	$40,000.00

[1] Actually, this "interest" is not really interest—it is additional premium (capital) that has been paid into the policy that *equals the interest* that was being paid to the finance company. That is the reason that it is adding to the cost basis of the policy. If you have trouble understanding this, go back to the grocery store on page 15. If you still don't understand, then contact me!

EQUIPMENT FINANCING ILLUSTRATION 2

START YEAR	AGE	NET ANN OUTLAY	ANNUAL LOAN	GROSS INTRST	CUM LOAN	TOTAL DIVID	NET CASH VALUE YR END	CUM NET OUTLAY	DEATH BENEFIT
1	30	$40,000	$0	$0	$0	$0	$24,029	$40,000	$1,342,420
2	31	$40,000	$0	$0	$0	$0	$65,282	$80,000	$1,448,237
3	32	$40,000	$0	$0	$0	$2,821	$109,637	$120,000	$1,565,319
4	33	$40,000	$0	$0	$0	$4,494	$157,363	$160,000	$1,684,787
5	34	-$34,600	$40,745	$2,784	$40,745	$6,339	$129,387	$125,400	$1,623,887
6	35	$18,000	-$12,551	$2,088	$28,194	$5,835	$155,945	$143,400	$1,613,616
7	36	$18,000	-$13,555	$1,084	$14,640	$6,641	$184,927	$161,400	$1,608,902
8	37	$18,000	-$14,639	$0	$1	$7,634	$216,568	$179,400	$1,609,727
9	38	-$34,600	$40,745	$2,784	$40,746	$8,750	$193,570	$144,800	$1,559,233
10	39	$18,000	-$12,550	$2,089	$28,195	$8,997	$225,539	$162,800	$1,563,333
11	40	$18,000	-$13,555	$1,084	$14,641	$10,172	$260,375	$180,800	$1,573,190
12	41	$18,000	-$14,639	$0	$2	$11,506	$298,379	$198,800	$1,588,842
13	42	-$34,600	$40,745	$2,784	$40,747	$13,022	$282,226	$164,200	$1,553,357
14	43	$18,000	-$12,550	$2,089	$28,196	$13,620	$321,600	$182,200	$1,573,180
15	44	$18,000	-$13,554	$1,085	$14,642	$15,196	$364,450	$200,200	$1,598,918
16	45	$18,000	-$14,639	$0	$3	$16,928	$411,071	$218,200	$1,630,573
17	46	-$34,600	$40,745	$2,784	$40,748	$18,838	$404,228	$183,600	$1,611,186
18	47	$18,000	-$12,550	$2,089	$28,198	$19,882	$453,637	$201,600	$1,647,702
19	48	$18,000	-$13,554	$1,085	$14,643	$21,920	$507,320	$219,600	$1,690,350
20	49	$18,000	-$14,639	$1	$5	$24,175	$565,630	$237,600	$1,739,228
21	50	-$34,600	$40,745	$2,784	$40,750	$26,643	$571,379	$203,000	$1,738,388
22	51	$18,000	-$12,550	$2,089	$28,200	$29,261	$634,365	$221,000	$1,795,515
23	52	$18,000	-$13,554	$1,085	$14,645	$32,025	$702,736	$239,000	$1,859,477
24	53	$18,000	-$14,638	$1	$7	$35,154	$776,947	$257,000	$1,930,588
25	54	-$34,600	$40,745	$2,785	$40,752	$38,604	$799,921	$222,400	$1,952,136
26	55	$18,000	-$12,550	$2,089	$28,202	$41,393	$881,561	$240,400	$2,031,725
27	56	$18,000	-$13,554	$1,085	$14,648	$45,296	$969,987	$258,400	$2,119,304
28	57	$18,000	-$14,638	$1	$10	$49,514	$1,065,819	$276,400	$2,214,986
29	58	-$34,600	$40,745	$2,785	$40,756	$54,105	$1,112,034	$241,800	$2,262,110
30	59	$18,000	-$12,550	$2,089	$28,206	$57,975	$1,218,591	$259,800	$2,368,087
31	60	$18,000	-$13,554	$1,085	$14,653	$62,989	$1,333,894	$277,200	$2,482,990
32	61	$18,000	-$14,638	$1	$15	$68,587	$1,458,494	$295,800	$2,607,224
33	62	-$34,600	$40,745	$2,785	$40,761	$74,535	$1,535,684	$261,200	$2,684,155
34	63	$18,000	-$12,549	$2,090	$28,211	$80,157	$1,675,538	$279,200	$2,821,850
35	64	$18,000	-$983	$2,017	$27,228	$87,071	$1,826,253	$297,200	$2,977,525
36	65	$18,000	-$17,262	$738	$9,966	$95,071	$1,988,254	$315,200	$3,158,537
37	66	-$100,000	-$9,966	$0	$0	$102,076	$2,035,134	$215,200	$3,164,149
38	67	-$125,000	$0	$0	$0	$104,516	$2,058,047	$90,200	$3,134,075
39	68	-$125,000	$0	$0	$0	$106,120	$2,082,100	-$34,800	$3,106,363
40	69	-$125,000	$0	$0	$0	$107,725	$2,107,133	-$159,800	$3,081,626
41	70	-$125,000	$0	$0	$0	$109,155	$2,133,392	-$284,800	$3,059,592
42	71	-$125,000	$0	$0	$0	$110,913	$2,160,972	-$409,800	$3,040,867
43	72	-$125,000	$0	$0	$0	$112,895	$2,189,983	-$534,800	$3,025,638
44	73	-$125,000	$0	$0	$0	$115,203	$2,220,485	-$659,800	$3,014,273
45	74	-$125,000	$0	$0	$0	$117,800	$2,252,578	-$784,800	$3,006,960
46	75	-$125,000	$0	$0	$0	$120,562	$2,286,240	-$909,800	$3,003,673
47	76	-$125,000	$0	$0	$0	$123,389	$2,321,397	-$1,034,800	$3,004,192
48	77	-$125,000	$0	$0	$0	$126,004	$2,358,074	-$1,159,800	$3,008,332
49	78	-$125,000	$0	$0	$0	$128,488	$2,396,400	-$1,284,800	$3,014,857
50	79	-$125,000	$0	$0	$0	$130,807	$2,436,406	$1,409,800	$3,024,486
51	80	-$125,000	$0	$0	$0	$133,068	$2,478,201	-$1,534,800	$3,036,856
52	81	-$125,000	$0	$0	$0	$135,414	$2,521,930	-$1,659,800	$3,052,142
53	82	-$125,000	$0	$0	$0	$137,995	$2,567,695	-$1,784,800	$3,070,705
54	83	-$125,000	$0	$0	$0	$140,948	$2,615,623	-$1,909,800	$3,093,000
55	84	-$125,000	$0	$0	$0	$144,273	$2,665,716	-$2,034,800	$3,119,289

EQUIPMENT FINANCING ILLUSTRATION 3

START YEAR	AGE	NET ANNUAL OUTLAY	ANNUAL LOAN	GROSS INTRST	CUM LOAN	TOTAL DIVID	NET CASH VALUE YR END	CUM NET OUT-LAY	DEATH BEN-EFIT
1	30	$40,000	$0	$0	$0	$0	$24,029	$40,000	$1,342,420
2	31	$40,000	$0	$0	$0	$0	$65,282	$80,000	$1,448,237
3	32	$40,000	$0	$0	$0	$2,821	$109,637	$120,000	$1,565,319
4	33	$40,000	$0	$0	$0	$4,494	$157,363	$160,000	$1,684,787
5	34	-$69,200	$81,490	$5,568	$81,490	$6,339	$91,595	$90,800	$1,596,709
6	35	$36,000	-$25,101	$4,177	$56,389	$5,313	$134,075	$126,800	$1,610,004
7	36	$36,000	-$27,109	$2,169	$29,279	$6,439	$180,536	$162,800	$1,631,380
8	37	$36,000	-$29,278	$0	$1	$7,873	$231,349	$198,800	$1,660,687
9	38	-$69,200	$81,490	$5,568	$81,491	$9,467	$171,834	$129,600	$1,584,168
10	39	$36,000	-$25,101	$4,177	$56,390	$9,261	$221,108	$165,600	$1,613,376
11	40	$36,000	-$27,109	$2,169	$29,281	$10,828	$274,921	$201,600	$1,650,787
12	41	$36,000	-$29,278	$0	$3	$12,680	$333,728	$237,600	$1,696,412
13	42	-$69,200	$81,490	$5,568	$81,793	$14,769	$282,831	$168,400	$1,636,439
14	43	$36,000	-$25,101	$4,177	$56,392	$15,015	$341,434	$204,400	$1,683,436
15	44	$36,000	-$27,109	$2,169	$29,284	$17,086	$405,335	$240,400	$1,738,864
16	45	$36,000	-$29,278	$0	$6	$19,437	$475,001	$276,400	$1,802,681
17	46	-$69,200	$81,490	$5,568	$81,496	$22,040	$435,842	$207,200	$1,761,096
18	47	$36,000	-$25,101	$4,177	$56,396	$22,857	$507,112	$243,200	$1,827,494
19	48	$36,000	-$27,109	$2,169	$29,287	$25,539	$584,685	$279,200	$1,902,686
20	49	$36,000	-$29,277	$1	$10	$28,551	$669,103	$315,200	$1,986,685
21	50	-$69,200	$81,490	$5,568	$81,500	$31,867	$645,844	$246,000	$1,966,756
22	51	$36,000	-$25,100	$4,178	$56,400	$34,433	$734,254	$282,000	$2,057,239
23	52	$36,000	-$27,108	$2,170	$29,291	$38,021	$830,372	$318,000	$2,157,433
24	53	$36,000	-$29,277	$1	$15	$42,139	$934,859	$354,000	$2,267,610
25	54	-$69,200	$81,491	$5,569	$81,505	$46,681	$933,323	$284,800	$2,274,318
26	55	$36,000	-$25,100	$4,178	$56,405	$49,694	$1,045,243	$320,800	$2,391,973
27	56	$36,000	-$27,108	$2,170	$29,298	$54,712	$1,166,639	$356,800	$2,520,871
28	57	$36,000	-$29,276	$2	$21	$60,214	$1,298,374	$392,800	$2,660,981
29	58	-$69,200	$81,491	$5,569	$81,512	$66,213	$1,326,108	$323,600	$2,698,970
30	59	$36,000	-$25,099	$4,179	$56,413	$70,604	$1,469,410	$359,600	$2,849,063
31	60	$36,000	-$27,107	$2,171	$29,306	$77,062	$1,624,655	$395,600	$3,011,471
32	61	$36,000	-$29,276	$2	$30	$84,338	$1,792,597	$431,600	$3,187,108
33	62	-$69,200	$81,492	$5,570	$81,522	$92,066	$1,859,294	$362,400	$3,262,028
34	63	$36,000	-$25,098	$4,180	$56,424	$98,685	$2,044,466	$398,400	$3,451,585
35	64	$36,000	-$18,166	$2,834	$38,258	$107,565	$2,244,289	$434,400	$3,661,236
36	65	$36,000	-$35,819	$181	$2,438	$117,620	$2,459,578	$470,400	$3,900,252
37	66	-$150,000	-$2,438	$0	$0	$126,929	$2,491,237	$320,400	$3,871,920
38	67	-$150,000	$0	$0	$0	$128,844	$2,522,477	$170,400	$3,840,316
39	68	-$150,000	$0	$0	$0	$131,038	$2,556,452	$20,400	$3,813,065
40	69	-$150,000	$0	$0	$0	$133,251	$2,591,986	-$129,600	$3,789,737
41	70	-$150,000	$0	$0	$0	$135,271	$2,629,408	-$279,600	$3,769,952
42	71	-$150,000	$0	$0	$0	$137,714	$2,668,859	-$429,600	$3,754,541
43	72	-$150,000	$0	$0	$0	$140,459	$2,710,504	-$579,600	$3,743,740
44	73	-$150,000	$0	$0	$0	$143,633	$2,754,446	-$729,600	$3,738,053
45	74	-$150,000	$0	$0	$0	$147,193	$2,800,838	-$879,600	$3,737,757
46	75	-$150,000	$0	$0	$0	$150,989	$2,849,686	-$1,029,600	$3,742,855
47	76	-$150,000	$0	$0	$0	$154,900	$2,900,930	-$1,179,600	$3,753,134
48	77	-$150,000	$0	$0	$0	$158,583	$2,954,635	-$1,329,600	$3,767,952
49	78	-$150,000	$0	$0	$0	$162,136	$3,010,996	-$1,479,600	$3,787,052
50	79	-$150,000	$0	$0	$0	$165,519	$3,070,088	-$1,629,600	$3,810,113
51	80	-$150,000	$0	$0	$0	$168,864	$3,132,087	-$1,779,600	$3,837,127
52	81	-$150,000	$0	$0	$0	$172,353	$3,197,214	-$1,929,600	$3,868,351
53	82	-$150,000	$0	$0	$0	$176,180	$3,265,639	-$2,079,600	$3,904,285
54	83	-$150,000	$0	$0	$0	$180,519	$3,337,566	-$2,229,600	$3,945,570
55	84	-$150,000	$0	$0	$0	$185,378	$3,413,042	-$2,379,600	$3,992,624

EQUIPMENT FINANCING ILLUSTRATION 4

START YEAR	AGE	NET ANNUAL OUTLAY	ANNUAL LOAN	GROSS INTRST	CUM LOAN	TOTAL DIVID	NET CASH VALUE YR END	CUM NET OUTLAY	DEATH BEN-EFIT
1	30	$40,000	$0	$0	$0	$0	$24,029	$40,000	$1,342,420
2	31	$40,000	$0	$0	$0	$0	$65,282	$80,000	$1,448,237
3	32	$40,000	$0	$0	$0	$2,821	$109,637	$120,000	$1,565,319
4	33	$40,000	$0	$0	$0	$4,494	$157,363	$160,000	$1,684,787
5	34	-$103,800	$122,279	$8,354	$122,279	$6,339	$53,805	$56,200	$1,569,672
6	35	$54,000	-$37,603	$6,272	$84,677	$4,795	$112,218	$110,200	$1,606,671
7	36	$54,000	-$40,611	$3,264	$44,066	$6,251	$176,148	$164,200	$1,654,271
8	37	$54,000	-$43,860	$15	$206	$8,108	$246,132	$218,200	$1,712,150
9	38	-$103,800	$122,296	$8,371	$122,502	$10,192	$150,101	$114,400	$1,609,788
10	39	$54,000	-$37,585	$6,290	$84,917	$9,539	$216,689	$168,400	$1,664,185
11	40	$54,000	-$40,592	$3,283	$44,326	$11,507	$289,480	$222,400	$1,729,279
12	41	$54,000	-$43,839	$36	$487	$13,871	$369,090	$276,400	$1,804,989
13	42	-$103,800	$122,318	$8,393	$122,805	$16,536	$283,426	$172,600	$1,720,717
14	43	$54,000	-$37,561	$6,314	$85,244	$16,411	$361,247	$226,600	$1,794,865
15	44	$54,000	-$40,565	$3,310	$44,679	$18,995	$446,189	$280,600	$1,880,059
16	45	$54,000	-$43,811	$64	$868	$21,970	$538,881	$334,600	$1,976,116
17	46	-$103,800	$122,348	$8,423	$123,216	$25,262	$467,377	$230,800	$1,912,504
18	47	$54,000	-$37,528	$6,347	$85,689	$25,850	$560,485	$284,800	$2,008,728
19	48	$54,000	-$40,530	$3,345	$45,159	$29,184	$661,926	$338,800	$2,116,514
20	49	$54,000	-$43,772	$103	$1,387	$32,964	$772,420	$392,800	$2,235,687
21	50	-$103,800	$122,390	$8,465	$123,776	$37,128	$720,124	$289,000	$2,196,833
22	51	$54,000	-$37,483	$6,392	$86,293	$39,649	$833,918	$343,000	$2,320,607
23	52	$54,000	-$40,482	$3,393	$45,812	$44,063	$957,733	$397,000	$2,457,048
24	53	$54,000	-$43,720	$155	$2,092	$49,169	$1,092,447	$451,000	$2,606,303
25	54	-$103,800	$122,446	$8,521	$124,538	$54,814	$1,066,331	$347,200	$2,598,277
26	55	$54,000	-$37,422	$6,453	$87,116	$58,041	$1,208,468	$401,200	$2,753,884
27	56	$54,000	-$40,416	$3,459	$46,700	$64,199	$1,362,758	$455,200	$2,924,080
28	57	$54,000	-$43,649	$226	$3,051	$70,982	$1,530,302	$509,200	$3,108,575
29	58	-$103,800	$122,522	$8,597	$125,573	$78,388	$1,539,451	$405,400	$3,137,471
30	59	$54,000	-$37,339	$6,536	$88,234	$83,309	$1,719,389	$459,400	$3,331,519
31	60	$54,000	-$40,326	$3,549	$47,907	$91,225	$1,914,427	$513,400	$3,541,718
32	61	$54,000	-$43,552	$323	$4,355	$100,161	$2,125,560	$567,400	$3,768,227
33	62	-$103,800	$122,626	$8,701	$126,981	$109,689	$2,181,595	$463,600	$3,841,078
34	63	$54,000	-$37,227	$6,648	$89,754	$117,310	$2,411,884	$517,600	$4,082,237
35	64	$54,000	-$34,940	$4,060	$54,814	$128,156	$2,660,604	$571,600	$4,345,617
36	65	$54,000	-$53,935	$65	$879	$140,279	$2,928,933	$625,600	$4,642,383
37	66	-$151,559	-$879	$0	$0	$151,891	$2,995,540	$474,041	$4,655,185
38	67	-$175,000	$0	$0	$0	$155,855	$3,041,115	$299,041	$4,628,831
39	68	-$175,000	$0	$0	$0	$158,863	$3,089,318	$124,041	$4,606,778
40	69	-$175,000	$0	$0	$0	$161,926	$3,139,976	-$50,959	$4,589,881
41	70	-$175,000	$0	$0	$0	$164,787	$3,193,525	-$255,959	$4,577,658
42	71	-$175,000	$0	$0	$0	$168,196	$3,250,179	-$400,959	$4,571,206
43	72	-$175,000	$0	$0	$0	$172,009	$3,310,184	-$575,959	$4,570,839
44	73	-$175,000	$0	$0	$0	$176,386	$3,373,702	-$750,959	$4,577,235
45	74	-$175,000	$0	$0	$0	$181,281	$3,440,980	-$925,959	$4,590,797
46	75	-$175,000	$0	$0	$0	$186,515	$3,512,072	-$1,100,959	$4,611,591
47	76	-$175,000	$0	$0	$0	$191,944	$3,586,953	-$1,275,959	$4,639,438
48	77	-$175,000	$0	$0	$0	$197,148	$3,665,756	-$1,450,959	$4,673,568
49	78	-$175,000	$0	$0	$0	$202,246	$3,748,778	-$1,625,959	$4,713,737
50	79	-$175,000	$0	$0	$0	$207,188	$3,836,167	-$1,800,959	$4,759,587
51	80	-$175,000	$0	$0	$0	$212,140	$3,928,201	-$1,975,959	$4,811,160
52	81	-$175,000	$0	$0	$0	$217,327	$4,025,219	-$2,150,959	$4,868,833
53	82	-$175,000	$0	$0	$0	$222,999	$4,127,498	-$2,325,959	$4,933,303
54	83	-$175,000	$0	$0	$0	$229,384	$4,235,359	-$2,500,959	$5,005,463
55	84	-$175,000	$0	$0	$0	$236,496	$4,348,931	-$2,675,959	$5,085,958

EQUIPMENT FINANCING ILLUSTRATION 5

START YEAR	AGE	NET ANNUAL OUTLAY	ANNUAL LOAN	GROSS INTRST	CUM LOAN	TOTAL DIVID	NET CASH VALUE YR END	CUM NET OUT-LAY	DEATH BENEFIT
1	30	$40,000	$0	$0	$0	$0	$24,029	$40,000	$1,342,320
2	31	$40,000	$0	$0	$0	$0	$65,282	$80,000	$1,448,237
3	32	$40,000	$0	$0	$0	$2,821	$109,637	$120,000	$1,565,319
4	33	$40,000	$0	$0	$0	$4,494	$157,363	$160,000	$1,684,787
5	34	-$103,800	$127,512	$8,712	$127,512	$6,339	$53,786	$56,200	$1,584,458
6	35	$54,000	-$31,919	$7,081	$95,593	$4,969	$112,061	$110,200	$1,635,969
7	36	$54,000	-$34,473	$4,527	$61,120	$6,583	$175,757	$164,200	$1,697,575
8	37	$54,000	-$37,230	$1,770	$23,890	$8,614	$245,396	$218,200	$1,768,944
9	38	-$103,800	$129,411	$10,611	$153,301	$10,883	$148,965	$114,400	$1,679,848
10	39	$54,000	-$29,856	$9,144	$123,445	$10,455	$214,962	$168,400	$1,746,776
11	40	$54,000	-$32,244	$6,756	$91,201	$12,634	$287,000	$222,400	$1,823,933
12	41	$54,000	-$34,824	$4,176	$56,377	$15,227	$365,675	$276,400	$1,911,188
13	42	-$207,600	$243,406	$20,806	$299,783	$18,142	$165,633	$68,800	$1,725,944
14	43	$108,000	-$76,457	$16,543	$223,326	$16,402	$290,187	$176,800	$1,853,241
15	44	$108,000	-$82,574	$10,426	$140,752	$19,912	$426,404	$284,800	$1,998,637
16	45	$108,000	-$89,180	$3,820	$51,572	$24,087	$575,362	$392,800	$2,161,421
17	46	-$207,600	$243,024	$20,424	$294,597	$28,742	$392,937	$185,200	$2,000,774
18	47	$108,000	-$76,872	$16,128	$217,724	$27,868	$536,501	$293,200	$2,154,448
19	48	$108,000	-$83,022	$9,978	$134,702	$32,286	$693,275	$401,200	$2,326,852
20	49	$108,000	-$89,664	$3,336	$45,038	$37,478	$864,418	$509,200	$2,517,248
21	50	-$207,600	$242,505	$19,905	$287,546	$43,207	$705,949	$301,600	$2,385,995
22	51	$108,000	-$77,437	$15,563	$210,106	$44,501	$875,358	$409,600	$2,572,699
23	52	$108,000	-$83,632	$9,369	$126,475	$50,269	$1,060,074	$517,600	$2,779,531
24	53	$108,000	-$90,322	$2,678	$36,153	$57,066	$1,261,471	$625,600	$3,006,024
25	54	-$207,600	$241,798	$19,198	$277,951	$64,602	$1,135,701	$418,000	$2,911,996
26	55	$108,000	-$78,204	$14,796	$199,747	$66,968	$1,340,515	$526,000	$3,137,814
27	56	$108,000	-$84,460	$8,540	$115,287	$74,866	$1,563,323	$634,000	$3,386,220
28	57	$108,000	-$91,217	$1,783	$24,070	$83,735	$1,805,783	$742,000	$3,656,122
29	58	-$207,600	$240,838	$18,238	$264,908	$93,461	$1,724,127	$534,400	$3,607,674
30	59	$108,000	-$79,247	$13,753	$185,660	$97,931	$1,976,257	$642,400	$3,881,313
31	60	$108,000	-$85,587	$7,413	$100,073	$108,018	$2,250,084	$750,400	$4,179,598
32	61	$108,000	-$92,434	$566	$7,639	$119,560	$2,547,145	$858,400	$4,501,938
33	62	-$207,600	$239,531	$16,931	$247,070	$131,924	$2,524,222	$650,800	$4,508,407
34	63	$108,000	-$80,666	$12,334	$166,504	$139,732	$2,839,460	$758,800	$4,841,208
35	64	$108,000	-$87,120	$5,880	$79,384	$153,454	$3,180,713	$866,800	$5,202,649
36	65	$79,384	-$79,384	$0	$0	$168,725	$3,518,411	$946,184	$5,575,034
37	66	-$225,000	$0	$0	$0	$183,274	$3,552,951	$721,184	$5,523,083
38	67	-$225,000	$0	$0	$0	$185,651	$3,589,023	$496,184	$5,463,109
39	68	-$225,000	$0	$0	$0	$188,259	$3,626,494	$271,184	$5,408,687
40	69	-$225,000	$0	$0	$0	$190,848	$3,665,965	$46,184	$5,359,300
41	70	-$225,000	$0	$0	$0	$193,119	$3,706,946	-$178,816	$5,314,244
42	71	-$225,000	$0	$0	$0	$195,938	$3,749,876	-$403,816	$5,274,745
43	72	-$225,000	$0	$0	$0	$199,128	$3,794,929	-$628,816	$5,241,036
44	73	-$225,000	$0	$0	$0	$202,861	$3,842,172	-$853,816	$5,213,776
45	74	-$225,000	$0	$0	$0	$207,068	$3,891,762	-$1,078,816	$5,193,283
46	75	-$225,000	$0	$0	$0	$211,532	$3,943,634	-$1,303,816	$5,179,468
47	76	-$225,000	$0	$0	$0	$216,080	$3,997,631	-$1,528,816	$5,171,970
48	77	-$225,000	$0	$0	$0	$220,234	$4,053,769	-$1,753,816	$5,169,749
49	78	-$225,000	$0	$0	$0	$224,131	$4,112,242	-$1,978,816	$5,172,389
50	79	-$225,000	$0	$0	$0	$227,716	$4,173,070	$2,203,816	$5,179,346
51	80	-$225,000	$0	$0	$0	$231,171	$4,236,411	-$2,428,816	$5,190,527
52	81	-$225,000	$0	$0	$0	$234,739	$4,302,479	-$2,653,816	$5,206,199
53	82	-$225,000	$0	$0	$0	$238,677	$4,371,713	-$2,878,816	$5,226,953
54	83	-$225,000	$0	$0	$0	$243,213	$4,443,395	-$3,103,816	$5,253,566
55	84	-$225,000	$0	$0	$0	$248,340	$4,518,391	-$3,328,816	$5,286,516

ADDENDUM

Since the initial publication of this book a number of people have expressed the concern that "the figures you are using in Equipment Financing are for the dividend scale of the year 2000 for that particular company. They are out of date. The dividend scales of most companies are *down* and will diminish the results." This is *true*, but I am afraid that these folks have missed the main point of creating your own banking *system*. A system consists of *many* life insurance policies and the number of years that each policy is *capitalized* must increase when interest rates go down, *if you are going to expect similar results as those depicted.*

Interest rates are a function of the market (Alan Greenspan attempts to manipulate the market) – they are up and they are down. Everyone in the financial services business *knows,* that in the Bond Market, when interest rates go *up* then the price (or value) of bonds goes *down, and vice versa.* And so, to generate a certain income (yield) from bonds, if interest rates go down, I must pay *more* capital into the bond. If rates go up, then I don't have to put as much money into the bond to generate the same income.

The same principle occurs in the Equipment Financing example. When interest rates go down (*a market function that you cannot control*) then you should *expect* to have to put in *more capital* in order to achieve the same results.

Look at illustration #6 on the following page where I ran the same policy but *capitalized the policy for five years* using a much more recent dividend scale with the same company. Now compare the results with illustration #2 on page 59. Please notice that the results are *considerably better*! If the businessman now financed more of his equipment through this policy, reason and logic tells you that the results *will be better* than those depicted in this book, assuming that he paid his own banking system the interest rates as those he was paying the finance company.

I sincerely hope that this exercise calms the fears that you may have about the validity of the *Infinite Banking Concept.* As stated at the outset of a presentation–"This is an exercise in IMAGINATION, REASON, LOGIC AND PROPHECY". None of the figures you are going to see are 'set in concrete.' They will vary with interest rates – and *how you treat the system. Your behavior* in managing the system is the most important factor in the entire equation." Capitalizing the policy 4 ½ years would probably still produce better results than the original illustration on page 59. Please, *use* your imagination!

Of course, the results are also affected by the "administrator" of the system (the Life Insurance Company). Some do a better job than others. If the company that you use does not measure up, then you might consider getting a contract with one that does.

EQUIPMENT FINANCING ILLUSTRATION 6

START YEAR	AGE	NET ANNUAL OUTLAY	ANNUAL LOAN	GROSS INTEREST	CUMULA-TIVE LOAN	TOTAL DIVI-DEND	NET CASH VALUE YR END	CUM NET OUTLAY	DEATH BEN-EFIT
1	29	$40,000	$0	$0	$0	$0	$24,541	$40,000	$1,403,457
2	30	$40,000	$0	$0	$0	$0	$65,620	$80,000	$1,516,989
3	31	$40,000	$0	$0	$0	$2,207	$109,396	$120,000	$1,635,990
4	32	$40,000	$0	$0	$0	$3,484	$156,096	$160,000	$1,756,876
5	33	$40,000	$0	$0	$0	$4,869	$206,137	$200,000	$1,880,115
6	34	-$34,600	$37,368	$2,768	$37,368	$6,632	$180,630	$165,400	$1,808,524
7	35	$18,000	-$24,551	$949	$12,817	$6,801	$210,176	$183,400	$1,771,204
8	36	$18,000	-$8,155	$345	$4,663	$7,293	$242,141	$201,400	$1,787,367
9	37	$18,000	-$4,663	$0	$0	$8,409	$276,653	$219,400	$1,818,463
10	38	-$34,600	$37,368	$2,768	$37,368	$9,756	$256,732	$184,800	$1,762,693
11	39	$18,000	-$24,551	$949	$12,817	$10,223	$292,242	$202,800	$1,745,264
12	40	$18,000	-$8,155	$345	$4,663	$11,001	$330,593	$220,800	$1,773,409
13	41	$18,000	-$4,663	$0	$0	$12,445	$372,341	$238,800	$1,815,364
14	42	-$34,600	$37,368	$2,768	$37,368	$14,535	$360,571	$204,200	$1,777,743
15	43	$18,000	-$24,551	$949	$12,817	$15,754	$405,213	$222,200	$1,783,177
16	44	$18,000	-$8,155	$345	$4,663	$17,306	$453,724	$240,200	$1,828,615
17	45	$18,000	-$4,663	$0	$0	$19,539	$506,330	$258,200	$1,887,254
18	46	-$34,600	$37,368	$2,768	$37,368	$22,072	$506,217	$223,600	$1,871,319
19	47	$18,000	-$24,551	$949	$12,817	$23,771	$563,337	$241,600	$1,901,374
20	48	$18,000	-$8,155	$345	$4,663	$25,806	$625,253	$259,600	$1,965,704
21	49	$18,000	-$4,663	$0	$0	$28,620	$691,217	$277,599	$2,042,166
22	50	-$34,600	$37,368	$2,768	$37,368	$31,744	$705,627	$242,999	$2,048,732
23	51	$18,000	-$24,551	$949	$12,817	$32,274	$778,213	$260,999	$2,104,251
24	52	$18,000	-$8,155	$345	$4,663	$36,975	$856,715	$278,999	$2,189,458
25	53	$18,000	-$4,663	$0	$0	$40,639	$941,458	$296,999	$2,286,518
26	54	-$34,600	$37,368	$2,768	$37,368	$44,741	$975,970	$262,399	$2,318,270
27	55	$18,000	-$24,551	$949	$12,817	$48,375	$1,070,135	$280,399	$2,402,053
28	56	$18,000	-$8,155	$345	$4,663	$52,207	$1,171,731	$298,399	$2,512,355
29	57	$18,000	-$4,663	$0	$0	$57,061	$1,281,230	$316,399	$2,634,626
30	58	-$34,600	$37,368	$2,768	$37,368	$62,355	$1,342,279	$281,799	$2,695,587
31	59	$18,000	-$24,551	$949	$12,817	$67,201	$1,464,462	$299,799	$2,810,753
32	60	$18,000	-$8,155	$345	$4,663	$71,858	$1,595,496	$317,799	$2,948,918
33	61	$18,000	-$4,663	$0	$0	$77,521	$1,736,051	$335,799	$3,098,549
34	62	-$34,600	$37,368	$2,768	$37,368	$83,910	$1,829,865	$301,199	$3,190,055
35	63	$18,000	-$24,551	$949	$12,817	$90,005	$1,987,205	$319,199	$3,338,653
36	64	$18,000	-$8,155	$345	$4,663	$96,686	$2,155,928	$337,199	$3,509,494
37	65	$18,000	-$4,663	$0	$0	$104,584	$2,206,714	$241,862	$3,515,868
38	66	-$93,337	$0	$0	$0	$98,693	$2,228,898	$116,862	$3,475,011
39	67	-$125,000	$0	$0	$0	$100,481	$2,252,210	-$8,138	$3,437,935
40	68	-$125,000	$0	$0	$0	$102,279	$2,276,353	-$133,138	$3,404,069
41	69	-$125,000	$0	$0	$0	$103,664	$2,301,672	-$258,138	$3,373,378
42	70	-$125,000	$0	$0	$0	$105,384	$2,327,945	-$383,138	$3,345,772
43	71	-$125,000	$0	$0	$0	$106,965	$2,355,526	-$508,138	$3,321,559
44	72	-$125,000	$0	$0	$0	$109,052	$2,384,133	-$633,138	$3,321,559
45	73	-$125,000	$0	$0	$0	$111,088	$2,414,122	-$758,138	$3,283,924
46	74	-$125,000	$0	$0	$0	$113,745	$2,445,259	-$883,138	$3,270,898
47	75	-$125,000	$0	$0	$0	$116,230	$2,477,806	-$1,008,138	$3,261,870
48	76	-$125,000	$0	$0	$0	$119,080	$2,511,801	-$1,133,138	$3,256,717
49	77	-$125,000	$0	$0	$0	$121,815	$2,546,929	-$1,258,138	$3,254,786
50	78	-$125,000	$0	$0	$0	$124,062	$2,583,658	-$1,383,138	$3,255,971
51	79	-$125,000	$0	$0	$0	$126,459	$2,622,025	-$1,508,138	$3,260,167
52	80	-$125,000	$0	$0	$0	$128,797	$2,662,129	-$1,633,138	$3,267,341
53	81	-$125,000	$0	$0	$0	$131,202	$2,704,101	-$1,758,138	$3,277,660
54	82	-$125,000	$0	$0	$0	$133,836	$2,747,995	-$1,883,138	$3,291,444
55	83	-$125,000	$0	$0	$0	$136,812	$2,793,475	-$2,008,138	$3,308,612
56	84	-$125,000	$0	$0	$0	$139,710	$2,840,986	-$2,133,138	$3,329,630

PART V - CAPITALIZING YOUR SYSTEM AND IMPLEMENTATION

Assuming that you are, by now, sufficiently convinced that this is a course of action that you would like to take, the question becomes, "How do I get started?" The most important word that comes to my mind is *desire*. Without it, you probably can't do it. Remember Parkinson's Law back in Part II - everyone is already spending all financial resources on what he thinks is best. There has got to be some honest introspection at this point and a commitment to "get out of financial prison" must be a burning passion.

This is going to require a change in priorities in life and recognizing that controlling the banking function *personally* is the most important thing that can be done in your financial world. I strongly recommend that you find a life insurance agent that is thoroughly familiar with *The Infinite Banking Concept* to act as your coach. In all probability such an agent will be thoroughly familiar with questionnaires that will help you find out just how you are spending money now and show you ways to re-direct that cash flow to build your banking system. Above all, you must be patient. It is going to take years to get started - and it needs to be a lifetime commitment.

It is much like developing a regimen of physical conditioning. You must evaluate your current condition, get a coach to design a program of exercise and see that you do it regularly. As you make progress the coach will make changes to improve your results. It works! Millions will attest to its effectiveness.

Organize (or join one already in existence) a "wealth club" that meets periodically. Here, you have the support of others that are working their way out of darkness. Be sure to include members that already have a good track record in practicing the principles of *The Infinite Banking Concept*. This is important because you need to surround yourself with others of like-minded understanding. You don't want to become a victim of feeling that you are "the lone ranger." We all need the nourishment of a favorable environment. No one elevates himself much above the environment in which he operates.

There is a superb game-board game available called "CASHFLOW' by Robert Kiyosaki. The address is listed in the book recommendations section in the back of this book. These are books that I strongly recommend for your on-going financial education. Get together with your wealth club members and play this game. You will be utterly amazed at what you will learn - things that are just not taught elsewhere. There is also a version for children called CASHFLOW FOR KIDS. Get this game and play it with your children and/or grandchildren. I have seen nothing that will improve their "financial IQ" more than this game. These are not cheap toys - they are the highest quality teaching materials. We live in a time where many people know the price of everything - but the value of nothing! These games are costly, but the value is far greater. People pay much more for a course in college or some other educational institution and it will have nowhere near the value that these games will have on the financial future of you and the ones you hold dear.

Above all, get started now. The longer you wait, the more you have penalized yourself. Review the first four parts of this book regularly. If you know what is happening, you will know what to do. The following chapters of this book will help in stimulating your imagination so that you can find sources of premium dollars to capitalize your system.

THE RETIREMENT TRAP!

A thought had been working in my mind for several years and I finally got around to putting it on paper. It was 1976—the so-called Bi-Centennial Year—and I penned these words on my birthday and put them into my personal file for posterity. "Social Security will fall, as have all socialist programs since time began. Before it falls, they will attempt to prop it up. The source of funds that they will use is the reserves of private pension plans and other government sanctioned schemes."

Most folks laughed at me, but it was less than a year before the first "trial balloon" went up suggesting that it was a possibility. Of course, it was shot down right away but there has been an accelerating realization that this *is going to happen* in the not too distant future. Regardless of the facts many will be caught by surprise. Witness the "surprise" by most people, particularly in government circles, that the Soviet Union "collapsed so quickly." That is not so! It was doomed to failure from the start because it was *operating from a faulty premise* that government knows how to order the lives of people better than do the people themselves.

To those who would listen I explained that all the government had to do was remind you, "Look, Doctor that $10,000 you put into your pension plan last year *was not your money, and you know it!* We admit that $5,000 was, but the *other $5,000 was simply taxes that you were going to have to pay* had we not granted you this privilege. We simply *deferred your taxation* until you withdraw money at retirement. Social Security was created for the 'common good.' Pension plans were created for the 'common good.' It is all a part of the same piece of cloth. You have done a good job of putting funds into your plan - but Social Security is in trouble. *We need our half of your plan now* to prop it up." There is not a thing you can do about it because *they created the scheme* and *they can - and will- change their minds.* Furthermore, they will always use the path of least resistance to accomplish whatever it is that they want to do. The easiest money that they can get to is the reserves on such plans. It is the largest block of securities that exists in the world.

Since 1976 there has been an increasing flood of articles explaining that Social Security is a fraud - the world's largest con-game! Others explain how the government is going to confiscate your pension plans, etc. It is axiomatic that any government sponsored program will always accomplish the opposite of the stated intent. Check any of them out over an extended period of time and see for yourself. The most dangerous thing you can do with money is put it into government sponsored schemes.

When government creates a problem (read onerous taxation) and then turns around and creates an exception to the problem they created (read tax-sheltered retirement plans, etc.) aren't you just a little bit suspicious that you are being manipulated?

No matter how much they try to disguise it with euphemisms, Socialism does not work and never will. Avoid all such programs like the plague. You will be glad that you did.

Down through all of history mankind has indulged in some pretty stupid ideas and it seems to take quite a number of years before one of them finally runs its course and collapses. Often it takes seventy or more years for reality to become apparent.

One that has the world in its grip at present is the idea of "retirement" or more precisely "The Pension Idea." Read the Bible carefully and you will find no such reference to "….. and so, Moses retired and lived happily afterward." I can find no reference to the concept throughout history until the time of Bismarck in Germany — the 1890s.

The whole idea was to get the older folks out of the work force in order to make room for the younger folks — because "there are not all that many jobs that are available." The idea of creativity was seemingly beyond their comprehension. Bill Gates and Sam Walton would have boggled their minds!

Pensions in America, as we know them today, began during World War II. Before that time the idea was practically non-existent. Everything was "frozen" during the war. When you went to buy gasoline it didn't matter how much money you had.

The limiting factor was the A, B, or C sticker on the windshield of your car. Some government bureaucrat determined how much you "needed." When the housewife went to buy groceries, there were "ration points" that determined how much meat she could buy, how much of the other staples of life, etc, etc." A Socialist's paradise!

The same idea applied to wages—they were "frozen." Under such an environment, how can you give someone a pay raise without "giving a pay raise?" *Benefits*, of course!! This was the genesis of retirement plans and health insurance plans. This was also a function of the IRS Code, which began in 1913.

The monster has accelerated and now the inevitable results are beginning to manifest themselves. Pension plans and all other such "IRS qualified plans" are self destructing. The stories are so plentiful that there is no point in identifying just a few. It is common knowledge and will become more apparent with the passage of time.

Not long after WWII, in 1950, Paul Poirot of the Foundation for Economic Education (FEE) wrote a little book, *The Pension Idea*, in which he demonstrated that the idea would never work. His prophecy is now apparent. The publication has been out of print for many years. I think it is so important for everyone to understand that *Infinite Banking Concepts* got permission from FEE to re-publish the booklet and we now offer it for sale on our website, www.infinitebanking.org. I urge financial services agents to buy this book in quantity and see that your clients read it. They need to know its message.

One caveat — when you get to the matter of life insurance in Paul's book, please bear in mind that he had limited knowledge of how dividend-paying life insurance works, nor was there any knowledge of *The Infinite Banking Concept*.

Furthermore, it appears to be an established fact that many people die shortly after they "retire." Mankind seems to need a purpose in life. Consider the case of John Templeton, the creator of The Templeton Fund. See page 37 for details. My mentor was Leonard E. Read, the founder of The Foundation for Economic Education, Inc., back in 1946. He died at age 85, in his sleep, the night before the semi-annual meeting of the foundation. He was "going to work" the next day.

And, then, consider the case of W. Edward Deming, the business consultant who taught the Japanese the idea of "quality." He went to Japan in 1950 and changed their world as a result of his teachings. When he came back to America many years later he became the darling of the business world — and rightly so. Deming died at age 93, still lecturing on The Fourteen Points that made him famous. They are as follows:

The Fourteen Points

1. Create constancy of purpose
2. Adopt a new philosophy
3. End the practice of purchasing at lowest prices
4. Institute leadership
5. Eliminate empty slogans
6. Eliminate numerical quotas
7. Institute on-the-job training
8. Drive out fear
9. Break down barriers between departments
10. Take action to accomplish the transformation
11. Improve constantly and forever the process of production and service
12. Cease dependence on mass inspection
13. Remove barriers to pride of workmanship
14. Retrain vigorously

The Seven Deadly Sins

1. Lack of constancy of purpose
2. Emphasizing short-term profits and immediate dividends
3. Evaluation of performance, merit rating, or annual review
4. Mobility of top management
5. Running a company only on visible figures
6. Excessive medical costs
7. Excessive costs of warranty (Cummings and Worley 1993, 328)

THE COST OF ACQUISITION

In a recent magazine advertisement the company was making a point that it took seven people to buy the hammer that was shown. The hammer cost $17. The *time* of the seven people cost $100! It is the first time I have ever seen the matter addressed in such a manner. This is a matter that should be addressed daily in all business situations.

Even more strange is that all businesses recognize the fact that finance of the business is necessary—but they never address the *cost of acquisition of finance!* Some time ago I spent two years of contacts with a medical department at a prominent university before they would admit that the fact was true! It is a very significant factor in a business venture and its cost is often startling. Organizations that are supported by contributions are perhaps the easiest ones to quantify this cost because of their objective. Free money isn't *free!* Donors have to be persuaded to participate. In many cases they spend eighty-five cents to raise a dollar! The most efficient ones spend at least fifteen cents.

In his book, *IACOCCA*, Lee Iacocca stated that he wouldn't have become involved with Chrysler had he known just how bad off they were. But once it happened, what do you do but the best that you know how. The only way he could see that would work was to get a government-backed loan. Now comes the hard part—*how do you get a government-backed loan?*

You start by gathering your highest paid executives, accountants and lawyers and they all set up camp in the high-rent district inside the Beltway in Washington for the purpose of courting Lobbyists. (Are you beginning to get the picture?) Months later they announced that they had succeeded in their mission and it was time to celebrate. Iacocca reminded them that they "only had the government-backed guarantee. Now we have to go to *the banks to get the money."* The negotiations here made the lobbying efforts look like child's play! It was much more difficult, time-consuming and thus, expensive. At the last minute the bankers always find that *we need one more pint of blood!* (Having been on the receiving end of such activity I found this to be very funny).

Once this was finally completed the Chrysler delegation wanted, once more, to celebrate. Iacocca then brought them face-to-face with the fact that the banks were not going to give them the money. They were going to get *one-third of the money—and a bank employee with a long title* whose sole function in life was to harass them during the period of the loan. When the next third was needed they had to go through more of the same. By the time the last third came around the Chrysler folks had received their *education in corporate finance!*

All of the above anecdote is the *cost of acquisition of finance.* The cost of finance, itself, was in addition to that. Question: Who paid for all this activity? Answer: Those who bought Chrysler cars, that's who!

If you are in command of the banking function you do not have to go through all this expensive erosion. *The Infinite Banking Concept* does exactly that! You can make timely decisions. There is *no cost of acquisition.* You are in competition with others who *must* go through the erosion that has been outlined. Guess who wins?

"BUT, I CAN GET A HIGHER RATE OF RETURN"

When first exposed to the rationale of *The Infinite Banking Concept* a person will almost always think— and often voice the thought, "but I can get a higher rate of return by investing in _____." Unfortunately that person has not understood the message! We are not addressing the *yield of an investment—we are* discussing *how you finance anything that you buy.* It is *always* better to finance it through your banking system than *out of your pocket.*

To demonstrate this principle, suppose that "A" invests $100,000 for one year and earns 20%:

Gross yield	$20,000
Less taxes (30%)	- $6,000
Net yield	$14,000

Suppose "B" builds cash values of $100,000 in his own *Infinite Banking Concept* (Dividend-paying life insurance) plan, then borrows it from his system for 8% and then makes the *same investment as "A" above.* The results are like this:

Gross yield	$20,000
Less interest paid to his banking system	- $8,000
Taxable gain	$12,000
Less taxes (30%)	- $3,600
Net yield	$8,400

BUT, in this case you must remember *who the characters are in the play.* "B" *also owns the policy to which interest is paid and earns the $8,000* on a non-taxed basis. So the total results are like this:

Net yield from the investment	$8,400
Net yield from his banking system	+ $8,000
Total yield	$16,400

This principle applies to any investment that you might make, so there is no way that a person can "get a higher rate of return" by ignoring the banking process! There is a delay in time while getting "the banking system" established, but once this is done, it is a "one-time only event." Anytime a person starts up a new business there is a delay in time before profitability commences. When a life insurance policy is created, that is the equivalent of starting a business that never existed before and the same phenomenon is inevitable.

It is just like a Trust Agreement. A trust has a Grantor, a Trustee, and a Beneficiary. The Grantor puts property into a trust. The Trustee takes possession and title to all the property in the trust. The Trustee puts the property to work for the benefit of the Grantor.

When income is earned, it all goes to the Trustee —but, the Trustee has an obligation to the Grantor to carry out the mission of the trust. In such an example you have never heard one say, "Look how much money that Trustee is making!" To the contrary, one says, "Look how well the Trustee is doing for the benefit of the Grantor and Beneficiary!" Otherwise, the Grantor would never put property into the trust!

The Grantor can certainly be a place where the Trustee puts property to work. In the case of a life insurance policy, the Owner of the policy outranks every other place that an insurance company must put money (the equity in the Owner's policy) to work.

For proof of this fact, go back and study the Equipment Financing section of this book.

A number of people have had trouble understanding that the interest "B" paid to the insurance company went to increase the cash value of his policy.

If that is a problem to you, please study the diagram on page 26. The company has to lend money from the pool to any number of places in order to eventually pay the promised death benefit. It matters little where they put the money to work. Loans to any of the sources will increase the cash value.

For even further amplification, please study the table below. Get out your highlighter and mark the spaces on the pages given. Page 54 illustrates the insurance company managing all the cash values.

Page 59 shows what happens when he finances a truck through the policy and pays $19,400 in interest to his policy. In the first example he has paid out more than the increase in cash value. That is because the company has still not absorbed all the cost of acquisition of the policy. This usually takes about 12 years. In the next example the cash value increased more than the interest he paid. In the last example the cash value increase was much greater than the interest he paid to his policy.

A word of clarification is necessary here. The "interest" he pays the policy is not really interest on the loan. It is additional *premium* that is equal to the amount of interest he is paying to the finance company. Please go back to page 58 and throughly understand this fact.

Earnings Went to Owner's Policy, Not the Insurance Company

Page 54	Line 4 NCV	$157,363		
ILLUSTRATION 1	Line 8 NCV	$201,772		
	Gain	$44,409		
Page 59	Line 4 NCV	$157,363		
ILLUSTRATION 2	Line 8 NCV	$216,568	Difference in Outlay	$19,400
	Gain	$59,205	Difference in Gain	$14,796
Page 54	Line 8 NCV	$201,772		
ILLUSTRATION 1	Line 12 NCV	$262,987		
	Gain	$61,215		
Page 59	Line 8 NCV	$216,568		
ILLUSTRATION 2	Line12 NCV	$298,379	Difference in Outlay	$19,400
	Gain	$81,811	Difference in Gain	$20,596
Page 54	Line 24 NCV	$618,942		
ILLUSTRATION 1	Line 28 NCV	$833,139		
	Gain	$214,197		
Page 59	Line 24 NCV	$776,947		
ILLUSTRATION 2	Line 28 NCV	$1,065,819	Difference in Outlay	$19,400
	Gain	$288,872	Difference in Gain	$74,675
NCV = Net Cash Value				

AN EVEN DISTRIBUTION OF AGE CLASSES

A good man leaves an inheritance for his children's children.
- Proverbs 13:22a

Back in the days of my work as a consulting forester I used to describe to clients the ultimate design of a forest management plan. For instance, suppose that you are an owner of 4,000 acres of such property and that we plan to grow trees on a 40-year rotation. So we divide the land into 40 compartments of 100 acres each for management purposes.

Each year we plan to harvest one compartment and replant it. Next year we select another compartment and harvest and replant it, etc. It will take us 40 years to achieve "an even distribution of age classes"— we have one compartment for each year in the rotation. About 25 years into the growth of each one we plan an improvement cutting— the removal of the less desirable trees. This brings in some income and enables the land to concentrate the growth potential on the better specimens. Five years later we do the same thing on the same compartment. And five years later we do the final "improvement cutting" on it. Notice that we are gradually removing inferior trees so that growth is concentrated on the superior ones. Then we let the remaining trees grow to the ultimate age of 40 years.

When the cycle of replanting begins, we start with about 500 trees per acre and when the last improvement cutting is done, we are down to about 85 per acre that become the ultimate harvest. So, each year there is a final harvest on one compartment and three improvement cuttings on other compartments—a total of four sources of income per year while having only one expense of replanting (other than general operational expense, taxes, fire protection for the whole forest, etc.).

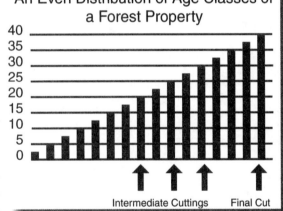

An Even Distribution of Age Classes of a Forest Property

Intermediate Cuttings   Final Cut

Once we have the whole system completely established it is a fabulous income producer, but it is going to take 40 years to get it done!

Something similar can be done with creating a "banking system" through life insurance and it can become vastly more profitable. But it is going to require a thorough knowledge of the concept. It all can work like the following example.

I know of a situation where an elderly couple (retired from business) were introduced to the idea of establishing substantial life insurance plans on their four grandchildren, two girls and two boys. The girls belonged to one of their sons and the boys belonged to the other son. The grandparents put $2,000 per year of premium into policies on each of the grandchildren, retaining ownership until their death, with ownership going to their sons at that time.

The sons are now grandparents and have a total of eight grandchildren collectively. They have diligently followed the example established by their parents, i.e. purchasing life insurance on each newborn in the amount of $2,000 annual premium. Premiums are planned for a payment period of 22 years (approximately one generation). Of course, the policies are designed according to the guidelines discussed back on page 38, that is, ones that emphasize cash accumulation and de-emphasize death benefit at the outset. So, after 22 years the "base premium" can be paid by dividends from the policy itself from that point forward. Surplus dividends buy additional paid-up insurance. The net effect of this is that the policy can be continued with no additional outlay, yet the face amount and cash values continue to grow very significantly over the years.

The mutual life insurance company that they are using illustrates the cash value at the grandson's age 22 to be $101,360. With no further outlay, the illustrated cash value at age 70 is $4,104,852. If the insured so desires, dividend withdrawals can be used for retirement purposes at this time in the amount of $225,000 per year and can be sustained at that level as long as the insured lives.

Suppose he dies at age 85. At that time he has recovered all the money that was paid into the policy ($44,000) plus $3,556,000 in income—and will still deliver $6,375,923 in death benefit to the next generation! I think that you will have to admit that this is impressive, but what you probably don't understand is this: if the insured, at age 22 will finance all his automobile purchases during lifetime from the cash values of the policy and "play the game," i.e., pay back to the policy the car payments that would have gone to a finance company, then the aforementioned cash values will be greater than depicted, and so will the retirement income figures! If he will finance his house purchases (when the cash values are adequate to do so) and pay back to the policy "closing costs" that would have had to be paid to a mortgage company, plus the monthly payments to amortize the mortgage (at the rates that they would require), then the figures cited will increase even more.

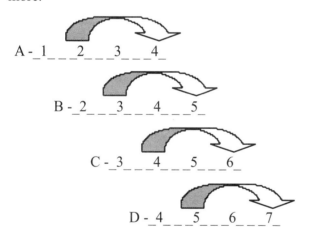

Beginning of cycle:
1- Senior Adult Generation - Age 66 - 88
2- Middle-Age Generation - Age 44 - 66
3- Child-Bearing Generation - Age 22 - 44
4- Birth to Adult Generation - Age 0 - 22

As each generation becomes grandparents, they buy life insurance on their grandchildren. If the message is passed on to each child-bearing generation—as they become grand-parents— then you can create the same effect as "the even distribution of age classes" in the growing trees, but it is far more profitable and certain as to the results. No forest fires. No plant diseases. No storms. No property taxes. You have created "perpetual motion" in your family's financial world!

There are a number of significant advantages to this plan:

- It covers multiple generations—promotes long range planning.

- Underwriting problems are minimized.

- Tax-free build-up of cash values over a long period of time.

- Outlay is very small compared with the ultimate yield.

- Generation paying the premiums can most easily afford them.

- When death benefit occurs, the system becomes self-sustaining.

- Precludes any need for Social Security.

- Passive income is assured.

- Estate planning is greatly simplified.

- Wealth "mentality" is transferred to succeeding generations over a long period of time to produce consistent understanding. They are learning a process—not buying a product.

- Promotes the understanding of what stewardship is all about.

Money won't buy happiness—but poor stewardship of money will steal happiness.

Be sure you know the condition of your flocks, give attention to your herds; for riches do not endure forever, and a crown is not secure for all generations.
-Proverbs 27:23-24

POLICY YEAR	AGE AT START OF YEAR	ANNUAL DIVI-DEND	NET PRE-MIUM	CUM NET PREMIUM	CUM NET A/T OUTLAY	BASE GUAR-ANTEED CASH VALUE	CASH VALUE OF ALL ADDS	NET CASH VALUE	NET DEATH BENEFIT
1	0	$0	$2,000	$2,000	$2,000	$0	$1,324	$1,324	$155,190
2	1	$0	$2,000	$4,000	$4,000	$0	$2,925	$2,925	$170,755
3	2	$196	$2,000	$6,000	$6,000	$0	$4,657	$4,657	$187,981
4	3	$276	$2,000	$8,000	$8,000	$0	$6,541	$6,541	$205,598
5	4	$373	$2,000	$10,000	$10,000	$0	$8,589	$8,589	$223,740
6	5	$477	$2,000	$12,000	$12,000	$548	$10,814	$11,362	$242,412
7	6	$583	$2,000	$14,000	$14,000	$1,125	$13,232	$14,357	$261,585
8	7	$697	$2,000	$16,000	$16,000	$1,733	$15,860	$17,593	$281,273
9	8	$817	$2,000	$18,000	$18,000	$2,373	$18,718	$21,090	$301,473
10	9	$951	$2,000	$20,000	$20,000	$3,040	$21,826	$24,866	$322,243
11	10	$1,099	$2,000	$22,000	$22,000	$3,737	$25,215	$28,951	$343,646
12	11	$1,265	$2,000	$24,000	$24,000	$4,456	$28,908	$33,364	$365,776
13	12	$1,456	$2,000	$26,000	$26,000	$5,193	$32,936	$38,129	$388,777
14	13	$1,677	$2,000	$28,000	$28,000	$5,941	$37,339	$43,281	$412,821
15	14	$1,941	$2,000	$30,000	$30,000	$6,700	$42,150	$48,850	$438,152
16	15	$2,235	$2,000	$32,000	$32,000	$7,463	$47,402	$54,865	$464,916
17	16	$2,561	$2,000	$34,000	$34,000	$8,234	$53,045	$61,279	$493,160
18	17	$2,827	$2,000	$36,000	$36,000	$9,018	$59,167	$68,185	$522,512
19	18	$3,168	$2,000	$38,000	$38,000	$9,817	$65,807	$75,623	$553,350
20	19	$3,526	$2,000	$40,000	$40,000	$10,640	$73,004	$83,645	$585,681
21	20	$3,892	$2,000	$42,000	$42,000	$11,348	$80,812	$92,160	$619,455
22	21	$4,277	$2,000	$44,000	$44,000	$12,084	$89,276	$101,360	$654,678
23	22	$4,681	$0	$44,000	$44,000	$12,855	$96,380	$109,235	$679,617
24	23	$5,015	$0	$44,000	$44,000	$13,662	$104,111	$117,773	$705,822
25	24	$5,383	$0	$44,000	$44,000	$14,509	$112,529	$127,038	$733,368
26	25	$5,774	$0	$44,000	$44,000	$15,396	$121,700	$137,096	$762,280
27	26	$6,204	$0	$44,000	$44,000	$16,326	$131,699	$148,025	$792,649
28	27	$6,677	$0	$44,000	$44,000	$17,297	$142,599	$159,896	$824,581
29	28	$7,205	$0	$44,000	$44,000	$18,310	$154,479	$172,789	$858,207
30	29	$7,783	$0	$44,000	$44,000	$19,363	$167,425	$186,788	$893,636
31	30	$8,418	$0	$44,000	$44,000	$20,460	$181,537	$201,997	$930,984
32	31	$9,121	$0	$44,000	$44,000	$21,594	$196,903	$218,498	$970,395
33	32	$9,886	$0	$44,000	$44,000	$22,772	$213,639	$236,412	$1,011,974
34	33	$10,721	$0	$44,000	$44,000	$23,988	$231,854	$255,842	$1,055,850
35	34	$11,635	$0	$44,000	$44,000	$25,246	$251,683	$276,928	$1,102,160
36	35	$12,632	$0	$44,000	$44,000	$26,542	$273,254	$299,797	$1,151,048
37	36	$13,723	$0	$44,000	$44,000	$27,880	$296,697	$324,577	$1,202,666
38	37	$14,905	$0	$44,000	$44,000	$29,255	$322,191	$351,446	$1,257,162
39	38	$16,206	$0	$44,000	$44,000	$30,668	$349,876	$380,544	$1,314,729
40	39	$17,616	$0	$44,000	$44,000	$32,119	$379,961	$412,080	$1,375,543
41	40	$19,165	$0	$44,000	$44,000	$33,607	$412,625	$446,232	$1,439,817
42	41	$20,844	$0	$44,000	$44,000	$35,129	$448,053	$483,182	$1,507,720
43	42	$22,657	$0	$44,000	$44,000	$36,689	$486,461	$523,150	$1,579,430
44	43	$24,618	$0	$44,000	$44,000	$38,284	$528,110	$566,394	$1,655,134
45	44	$26,739	$0	$44,000	$44,000	$39,918	$573,233	$613,151	$1,735,025
46	45	$29,028	$0	$44,000	$44,000	$41,585	$622,044	$663,630	$1,819,289
47	46	$31,482	$0	$44,000	$44,000	$43,292	$674,875	$718,168	$1,908,095
48	47	$34,113	$0	$44,000	$44,000	$45,035	$732,011	$777,046	$2,001,647
49	48	$36,969	$0	$44,000	$44,000	$46,819	$793,811	$840,630	$2,100,213
50	49	$40,049	$0	$44,000	$44,000	$48,639	$860,542	$909,181	$2,204,006

MALE, AGE 0, $139,896 Whole Life 100 Premium $600.00

Paid-Up Insurance Rider $1,400.00

Total Premium $2,000.00

POLICY YEAR	AGE AT START OF YEAR	ANNUAL DIVI-DEND	NET PRE-MIUM	CUM NET PREMIUM	CUMULA-TIVE NET A/T OUTLAY	BASE GUAR-ANTEED CASH VALUE	CASH VALUE OF ALL ADDS	NET CASH VALUE	NET DEATH BENEFIT
51	50	$43,344	$0	$44,000	$44,000	$50,497	$983,174	$983,174	$2,313,302
52	51	$46,941	$0	$44,000	$44,000	$52,388	$1,010,601	$1,062,989	$2,428,502
53	52	$50,888	$0	$44,000	$44,000	$54,312	$1,094,675	$1,148,987	$2,549,988
54	53	$55,120	$0	$44,000	$44,000	$56,262	$1,185,438	$1,241,700	$2,678,188
55	54	$59,812	$0	$44,000	$44,000	$58,236	$1,283,399	$1,341,635	$2,813,710
56	55	$64,959	$0	$44,000	$44,000	$60,232	$1,388,964	$1,449,196	$2,956,929
57	56	$70,376	$0	$44,000	$44,000	$62,250	$1,502,669	$1,564,919	$3,108,116
58	57	$76,218	$0	$44,000	$44,000	$64,291	$1,625,053	$1,689,344	$3,267,628
59	58	$82,421	$0	$44,000	$44,000	$66,354	$1,756,817	$1,823,171	$3,435,896
60	59	$89,167	$0	$44,000	$44,000	$68,441	$1,898,438	$1,966,879	$3,613,266
61	60	$96,225	$0	$44,000	$44,000	$70,548	$2,050,512	$2,121,060	$3,800,005
62	61	$103,774	$0	$44,000	$44,000	$72,670	$2,213,662	$2,286,333	$3,996,596
63	62	$111,885	$0	$44,000	$44,000	$74,802	$2,388,590	$2,463,392	$4,203,670
64	63	$120,679	$0	$44,000	$44,000	$76,937	$2,576,387	$2,653,324	$4,422,287
65	64	$130,520	$0	$44,000	$44,000	$79,069	$2,777,421	$2,856,490	$4,653,121
66	65	$140,814	$0	$44,000	$44,000	$81,196	$2,992,671	$3,073,866	$4,896,763
67	66	$151,933	$0	$44,000	$44,000	$83,315	$3,223,199	$3,306,514	$5,154,147
68	67	$164,001	$0	$44,000	$44,000	$85,430	$3,469,947	$3,555,378	$5,426,052
69	68	$176,840	$0	$44,000	$44,000	$87,541	$3,733,458	$3,820,999	$5,712,588
70	69	$189,936	$0	$44,000	$44,000	$89,650	$4,015,202	$4,104,852	$6,014,637
71	70	$204,377	-$225,000	-$181,000	-$181,000	$91,745	$4,074,061	$4,165,806	$5,986,001
72	71	$207,320	-$225,000	-$406,000	-$406,000	$93,821	$4,135,769	$4,229,591	$5,963,289
73	72	$211,264	-$225,000	-$631,000	-$631,000	$95,864	$4,200,502	$4,296,365	$5,947,320
74	73	$215,796	-$225,000	-$856,000	-$856,000	$97,857	$4,268,421	$4,366,278	$5,938,717
75	74	$220,951	-$225,000	-$1,081,000	-$1,081,000	$99,795	$4,339,728	$4,439,523	$5,937,788
76	75	$226,429	-$225,000	-$1,306,000	-$1,306,000	$101,671	$4,414,306	$4,515,977	$5,944,451
77	76	$231,970	-$225,000	-$1,531,000	-$1,531,000	$103,487	$4,492,315	$4,595,802	$5,958,385
78	77	$237,417	-$225,000	$1,756,000	$1,756,000	$105,254	$4,573,734	$4,678,987	$5,979,015
79	78	$242,546	-$225,000	-$1,981,000	-$1,981,000	$106,978	$4,658,850	$4,765,829	$6,005,762
80	79	$247,396	-$225,000	-$2,206,000	-$2,206,000	$108,471	$4,747,712	$4,856,383	$6,038,253
81	80	$252,127	-$225,000	-$2,431,000	-$2,431,000	$110,328	$4,840,645	$4,950,973	$6,076,580
82	81	$257,137	-$225,000	-$2,656,000	-$2,656,000	$111,942	$4,938,000	$5,049,942	$6,121,203
83	82	$262,681	-$225,000	-$2,881,000	-$2,881,000	$113,500	$5,039,995	$5,153,495	$6,172,852
84	83	$268,975	-$225,000	-$3,106,000	-$3,106,000	$114,989	$5,147,339	$5,261,998	$6,232,416
85	84	$276,137	-$225,000	-$3,331,000	-$3,331,000	$116,399	$5,259,052	$5,375,451	$6,300,144
86	85	$283,517	-$225,000	-$3,556,000	-$3,556,000	$117,734	$5,376,063	$5,493,796	$6,375,923
87	86	$290,888	-$225,000	-$3,781,000	-$3,781,000	$118,998	$5,498,257	$5,617,256	$6,459,421
88	87	$298,057	-$225,000	-$4,006,000	-$4,006,000	$120,211	$5,625,945	$5,746,156	$6,550,259
89	88	$304,994	-$225,000	-$4,231,000	-$4,231,000	$121,386	$5,759,473	$5,880,859	$6,647,902
90	89	$311,539	-$225,000	-$4,456,000	-$4,456,000	$122,549	$5,899,538	$6,022,087	$6,752,066
91	90	$317,956	-$225,000	-$4,681,000	-$4,681,000	$123,721	$6,047,362	$6,171,083	$6,862,669
92	91	$324,412	-$225,000	-$4,906,000	-$4,906,000	$124,937	$6,204,334	$6,329,271	$6,979,688
93	92	$330,958	-$225,000	-$5,131,000	-$5,131,000	$126,212	$6,372,607	$6,498,739	$7,103,273
94	93	$337,786	-$225,000	-$5,356,000	-$5,356,000	$127,658	$6,554,776	$6,682,434	$7,233,696
95	94	$345,039	-$225,000	-$5,581,000	-$5,581,000	$129,244	$6,754,156	$6,883,400	$7,372,182
96	95	$353,718	-$225,000	-$5,806,000	-$5,806,000	$131,011	$6,973,987	$7,104,995	$7,520,752
97	96	$364,600	-$225,000	-$6,031,000	-$6,031,000	$132,935	$7,216,844	$7,349,779	$7,682,264
98	97	$378,555	-$225,000	-$6,258,000	-$6,258,000	$134,962	$7,482,925	$7,617,887	$7,858,655
99	98	$394,710	-$225,000	-$6,481,000	-$6,481,000	$136,930	$7,762,225	$7,899,155	$8,047,298
100	99	$408,616	-$225,000	-$6,706,000	-$6,706,000	$139,896	$8,046,006	$8,185,902	$8,185,903

A DIFFERENT LOOK AT THE MONETARY VALUE OF A COLLEGE DEGREE

 Some thirty-six years ago, when I was just getting established in the Life Insurance business we were, of course, all thoroughly indoctrinated with "needs" selling. One of those "needs" was funding for college education for the client's children. It was all assumed that the children would go to college. If there was any question as to the value in monetary terms of doing so, we were taught to point out "how much more the average college educated child would earn over a lifetime of work compared with the average child who did not get the college degree." I forget what the figure tossed around at that time was, but in recent days I was remembering that mental exercise and decided to revisit the assumption.

First of all, I have the distinct feeling that the *college degree* is extremely over-rated in its value. Witness the number of people you know who have a degree and, thus, feel that they are *educated* but other than the degree there is very little evidence of the fact.

In a recent issue of a publication at Auburn University, Dr. Herbert Rotfeld, a professor in the Department of Marketing and Transportation had this to say:

> "I entered a doctoral program because of a deep and intense curiosity, a love of learning and a pathological enjoyment of reading. Today, as an educator, I want to inspire students to learn, to teach my students so they could teach others. But since the subject of my scholarly passion is business, my students only want what they see as job certification. Many want credits but don't want to learn.
>
> Since learning requires involvement of the students, a basic problem of modern education is the students who don't want to be in school. High school is something to be endured; they go to college only because a parent or school counselor told them to go. Unfortunately, as students are told to go to school, it is never emphasized that learning itself has value.
>
> Today, even doctoral students go to school not to learn, but to get certified, so it should not be a surprise that so many graduates at any level fail to exhibit interest or inspiration in learning.
>
> And many faculty believe that business practitioners have more credibility than anyone on campus. It is amazing how many people got into business education not because of a love of scholarship but because they were not very successful as business professionals. Now some former practitioners can be (and are) very respected scholars. Shifting from business practice to education can be a satisfying shift of career.
>
> But it is a business school, not a business. Too many former business practitioners do not do any new thinking once they leave the business world, talk of training students (for the jobs they themselves once held) and demand that as business educators who 'worked' they deserve a status they never possessed in business. These men and women never learned to think and do not expect such strange behavior from students. It is no surprise that the graduates, like faculty, often leave with a world view as expansive as that of a pet goldfish."

Professor Rotfeld went on to quote IBM chief executive Louis V. Gerstner, Jr. at a two-day national education summit in Palisades, NY; "business leaders do not (and should not) want business education to be vocationally oriented. It is not in the interest of business leaders to turn public schools into vocational schools. We can teach them how to read balance sheets. What is killing us is having to teach them to read and compute and communicate and to think."

Rotfeld concludes his article by saying, "I await the time when business education will be a respected activity for a hard working scholar, instead of a training ground for future anti-intellectuals and home for retired executives who came to campus so they could themselves quit thinking."

The above is a pretty strong statement about the condition of "higher education" in America, isn't it? And people are paying ever-increasing college costs to get a degree that is becoming less valuable. Dr. George Roche, former President of Hillsdale College has a lot to say about this phenomenon in his book, *The Fall of the Ivory Tower*. If you have not done so, I urgently recommend that you read this book. One of these days the consumers are going to wise up to the fact they have been conned and the "house of cards" is going to come crashing down. When the perceived value of anything has no real basis, a return to reality is inevitable.

A lot of the idea that *everybody needs a college education* has its roots in the period just after WWII with the advent of the GI Bill. Here came the huge number of "students" to get their degrees, when the major reason for this event was the fear of government powers that "all these servicemen returning to civilian life are going to wreck the economy. We have to do something with them." Since that time Parkinson's Law has taken effect — a luxury once enjoyed, becomes a necessity. And so, now the cry is that "everybody *deserves* a college education!" Please notice that the cost of doing so has risen much faster than inflation in the rest of the economy. This is always the pattern when government gets involved in anything. Let's contrast this phenomenon with that of the development of the Personal Computer, a field in which government has had a minimum of meddling (that is, until early December 1997 re: Microsoft Internet Explorer). Quality and performance have increased so rapidly that whatever you now have is obsolete within a year or so and the prices have gone down dramatically.

So much for the major reason for looking askance at the value of a college degree. Now let's look at the *monetary value* of the college degree as compared with an alternative—teaching the child the value of learning banking through the use of dividend-paying whole life insurance. To do so, I am not going to put a monetary value on the degree as *was* done in our presentations some 30-odd years ago. I am going to let you decide for yourself as to what a reasonable figure might be. Just compare that figure with the results of my recent study using a major mutual company's illustration software to construct the case for learning banking instead.

First, I assumed that the usual cost of the college degree is $20,000 per year for four years. From what information I can gather that seems to be the case. So I used this same figure to put into a high-premium policy, in this case $6,500 to a base Life Paid-Up at 65 policy plus $13,500 into a Paid-Up Additions Rider on an 18 year old male. This premium total of $20,000 was used to pay four annual premiums of $20,000 each. After the four years dividends were used to pay the base premium for the duration of the policy—the classical "premium offset" illustration—and so there was no further outlay.

Next, I assumed the Insured retired at age 70 (I no longer let people get away with the assumption of age 65 for retirement. *It is just not going to work in the future*) and surrendered dividend credits from that point on. Based on the current dividend scale of this company the cash values at age 70 were illustrated to be $2,457,303. Withdrawing dividend credits alone of $145,000 per year for retirement purposes could be sustained indefinitely. And assuming the Insured lived until age 85 means that he had withdrawn an income total of $2,175,000. If he died at that time the projected death benefit is $3,279,018. In all honesty, I don't believe that the college degree would produce comparable *financial* results. This scenario assumed that the Insured simply let the insurance company manage the cash values throughout the entire illustration.

If the Insured were taught to finance his automobile purchases through the policy ($21,450 financing package every four years, beginning at the first of the 5th year) and *paid back to the policy* that which he would have had to pay a finance company (6,500 per year for four years), then the results improve significantly. In this case, $2,698,593 in cash value, and the income from dividends could be increased to $150,000 per year (total income of $2,250,000 by age 85) plus a death benefit of $3,848,202 if death occurred at that time. In this example there were *no policy loans* at all. The $21,450 "automobile financing" packages were all *withdrawals* of dividend credits. The "repayments" were actually premiums to the base policy.

By the way, if the Insured was female, the above

results improve even more—in this case $2,959,517 cash value at age 70, dividend income of $150,000 per year ($2,250,000 in income by age 85) plus a death benefit of $5,233,432 if death occurred at age 85. The death benefit continues to increase if death occurs later.

So, in evaluating just the *financial benefits* of the college degree at a cost of $80,000 vs. putting that same $80,000 into high-premium whole life insurance, I don't believe the degree is as valuable. As a matter of fact, the probability of the college-educated person ever learning the benefits of "banking" through the use of whole life insurance is not very good. He will be exposed to some professor teaching him that "whole life insurance is a very poor place to put money." It will take a lot of effort to get this notion out of his head, because "unlearning" is more difficult than learning. I think that Professor Rotfeld might explain it, "He has been *trained* instead of having learned to *think*. Please remember that I am not against *higher education*. To the contrary, I believe it should be a life-long activity. But observation leads me to conclude that we have a lot of people in America with *degrees*—but not many of them are educated.

Following the illustration on JOHN Q. STUDENT is an illustration on SUSIE Q. STUDENT. Susie doesn't go to Vanderbilt (or some other college of equal stature) and then to medical school.

It is very apparent that a large proportion of medical students today is female. Note that spending the money to teach Susie "banking" through the use of dividend-paying life insurance instead of sending her to Vanderbilt and then to medical school:

- Eliminates the need for expensive malpractice insurance that is essential in a medical practice.
- Eliminates the need to establish a retirement plan of any kind.
- Eliminates the concern for whether Social Security will survive or not (it won't!).
- If she is determined to be around the medical community, all she has to do at the end of the eighth year is call the life insurance company and borrow enough money (she has access to $339,713 at the time) to buy eight luxury cars—take them down to the medical school and lease them to the professors there—because all of them drive that sort of car—and most all of them are leased

from some source. Eight months later she can add another car to the fleet just from lease income. Seven months later—another. Six months later—another, etc. In a short while she can enjoy a very good income just from the leasing business—in addition to the figures you see.

POL YR	AGE AT START YR	ANNUAL DIVI-DEND	NET PRE-MIUM	CUM NET PRE-MIUM	GUARANTEED CASH VALUE	CASH VALUE OF ALL ADDS	NET CASH VALUE	NET DEATH BENEFIT
1	18	$0	$20,000	$20,000	$0	$13,203	$13,203	$865,120
2	19	$0	$20,000	$40,000	$4,560	$28,347	$32,908	$949,534
3	20	$1,554	$20,000	$60,000	$9,284	$44,914	$54,198	$1,041,469
4	21	$2,523	$20,000	$80,000	$14,195	$63,010	$77,205	$1,136,779
5	22	$3,546	-$14,950	$65,050	$19,331	$45,758	$65,089	$1,028,821
6	23	$2,937	$6,500	$71,550	$24,701	$50,528	$75,229	$1,046,010
7	24	$3,362	$6,500	$78,050	$30,335	$55,924	$86,258	$1,065,100
8	25	$3,811	$6,500	$84,550	$36,234	$62,021	$98,255	$1,086,082
9	26	$4,315	-$14,950	$69,600	$42,413	$45,711	$88,124	$994,667
10	27	$3,826	$6,500	$76,100	$48,872	$51,580	$100,452	$1,014,440
11	28	$4,371	$6,500	$82,600	$55,604	$58,261	$113,855	$1,036,310
12	29	$4,976	$6,500	$89,100	$62,608	$65,840	$128,448	$1,050,410
13	30	$5,638	-$14,950	$74,150	$69,892	$51,289	$121,181	$956,291
14	31	$5,411	$6,500	$80,650	$77,440	$59,240	$136,681	$1,010,833
15	32	$6,227	$6,500	$87,150	$85,269	$66,350	$153,620	$1,038,159
16	33	$7,114	$6,500	$93,650	$93,378	$76,730	$172,108	$1,058,355
17	34	$8,076	-$14,950	$78,700	$101,752	$67,273	$169,025	$1,013,435
18	35	$8,052	$6,500	$85,200	$110,414	$78,649	$189,063	$1,045,462
19	36	$9,112	$6,500	$91,700	$119,355	$91,533	$210,888	$1,080,462
20	37	$10,248	$6,500	$98,200	$128,554	$105,030	$234,633	$1,118,589
21	38	$11,491	-$14,950	$83,250	$137,706	$99,163	$236,889	$1,032,750
22	39	$11,745	$6,500	$89,750	$147,107	$115,560	$262,655	$1,123,650
23	40	$13,105	$6,500	$95,250	$156,764	$133,919	$291,683	$1,167,845
24	41	$14,576	$6,500	$102,750	$165,653	$154,424	$231,083	$1,215,432
25	42	$16,160	-$14,950	$87,800	$176,827	$154,024	$330,851	$1,198,704
26	43	$16,774	$6,500	$94,300	$187,247	$177,464	$364,711	$1,250,092
27	44	$18,523	$6,500	$100,800	$197,932	$203,487	$401,419	$1,305,084
28	45	$20,406	$6,500	$107,300	$208,881	$232,278	$441,159	$1,363,808
29	46	$22,420	-$14,950	$92,350	$220,103	$240,860	$460,963	$1,366,514
30	47	$23,478	$6,500	$98,850	$231,605	$274,001	$505,607	$1,430,054
31	48	$25,724	$6,500	$105,350	$243,395	$310,420	$553,815	$1,497,589
32	49	$28,045	$6,500	$111,850	$255,473	$350,342	$605,815	$1,569,035
33	50	$30,535	-$14,950	$96,900	$267,855	$370,897	$638,752	$1,591,501
34	51	$32,140	$6,500	$103,433	$280,501	$416,927	$697,428	$1,668,663
35	52	$35,033	$6,500	$109,900	$293,427	$467,257	$760,684	$1,750,327
36	53	$38,130	$6,500	$116,400	$306,632	$522,288	$828,891	$1,836,726
37	54	$41,556	-$14,950	$101,450	$320,011	$559,238	$879,249	$1,881,997
38	55	$44,196	$6,500	$107,950	$333,669	$622,908	$956,576	$1,975,627
39	56	$48,068	$6,500	$114,450	$347,576	$692,227	$1,039,803	$2,075,753
40	57	$52,231	$6,500	$120,950	$361,755	$767,588	$1,129,342	$2,181,647
41	58	$56,667	-$14,950	$106,000	$376,222	$826,324	$1,202,546	$2,251,168
42	59	$60,346	$6,500	$112,500	$390,977	$913,265	$1,304,241	$2,367,211
43	60	$65,298	$6,500	$119,000	$406,043	$1,007,397	$1,413,440	$2,489,573
44	61	$70,601	$6,500	$125,500	$421,413	$1,109,181	$1,530,593	$2,618,549
45	62	$76,295	-$14,950	$110,550	$437,071	$1,196,028	$1,633,099	$2,716,268
46	63	$81,339	$6,500	$117,050	$453,124	$1,313,158	$1,766,182	$2,857,688

POL YR	AGE AT START YR	ANNUAL DIVI-DEND	NET PRE-MIUM	CUM NET PRE-MIUM	GUARANTEED CASH VALUE	CASH VALUE OF ALL ADDS	NET CASH VALUE	NET DEATH BENEFIT
47	64	$88,142	$6,500	$123,550	$469,273	$1,439,443	$1,908,716	$3,007,311
48	65	$95,278	$0	$123,550	$480,075	$1,571,223	$2,051,298	$3,165,315
49	66	$98,647	-$21,450	$102,100	$490,845	$1,689,950	$2,180,796	$3,290,454
50	67	$105,408	$0	$102,100	$501,585	$1,840,651	$2,342,236	$3,457,574
51	68	$113,726	$0	$102,100	$512,309	$2,002,208	$2,514,516	$3,634,022
52	69	$122,204	$0	$102,100	$523,009	$2,175,584	$2,698,593	$3,819,654
53	70	$131,557	-$150,000	-$47,900	$533,655	$2,200,046	$2,733,701	$3,792,211
54	71	$133,230	-$150,000	-$197,900	$544,200	$2,226,093	$2,770,293	$3,767,756
55	72	$135,539	-$150,000	-$347,900	$554,574	$2,253,878	$2,808,452	$3,747,076
56	73	$138,211	-$150,000	-$497,900	$564,698	$2,283,553	$2,848,251	$3,730,532
57	74	$141,265	-$150,000	-$647,900	$574,543	$2,315,250	$2,889,793	$3,718,495
58	75	$144,503	-$150,000	-$797,900	$584,068	$2,348,903	$2,932,971	$3,711,049
59	76	$147,754	-$150,000	-$947,900	$593,298	$2,384,568	$2,977,866	$3,708,057
60	77	$150,918	-$150,000	-$1,097,900	$602,263	$2,422,179	$3,024,442	$3,709,260
61	78	$153,845	-$150,000	-$1,247,900	$611,033	$2,461,833	$3,072,866	$3,714,229
62	79	$156,565	-$150,000	-$1,397,900	$619,625	$2,503,519	$3,123,144	$3,722,590
63	80	$159,180	-$150,000	-$1,547,900	$628,037	$2,547,417	$3,175,454	$3,734,120
64	81	$161,945	-$150,000	-$1,697,900	$636,240	$2,593,748	$3,229,987	$3,748,921
65	82	$165,020	-$150,000	-$1,847,900	$644,154	$2,642,687	$3,286,841	$3,767,292
66	83	$168,541	-$150,000	-$1,997,900	$651,711	$2,694,506	$3,346,216	$3,789,692
67	84	$172,577	-$150,000	-$2,147,900	$658,878	$2,749,202	$3,408,080	$3,816,651
68	85	$176,712	-$150,000	-$2,297,900	$665,649	$2,806,711	$3,472,359	$3,848,202
69	86	$180,800	-$150,000	-$2,447,900	$672,077	$2,867,086	$3,539,163	$3,884,210
70	87	$184,720	-$150,000	-$2,597,900	$678,233	$2,930,426	$3,608,659	$3,924,413
71	88	$188,454	-$150,000	-$2,747,900	$684,209	$2,996,830	$3,681,040	$3,968,536
72	89	$191,903	-$150,000	-$2,897,900	$690,108	$3,066,608	$3,756,716	$1,016,196
73	90	$195,234	-$150,000	-$3,047,900	$696,069	$3,140,354	$3,836,423	$1,067,205
74	91	$198,552	-$150,000	-$3,197,900	$702,241	$3,218,755	$3,920,996	$4,121,488
75	92	$201,889	-$150,000	-$3,347,900	$408,817	$3,302,854	$4,011,471	$4,178,991

MALE, AGE 18, Life Paid-up at Age 65 $778,218
PREFERRED $6,500
Paid-Up Additions Rider $13,500
Total Premium $20,000

① $20,000 represents premiums going to life insurance policy instead of going to the cost of getting a degree.

② -$14,950 represents an automobile purchase of $21,450 less a payment of $6,500 to premium instead of to a finance company or bank.

③ $6,500 represents a premium payment instead of a car payment to a bank.

④ $2,698,593 is the illustrated cash value at age 70.

⑤ -$150,000 represents annual income from dividends at retirement time.

⑥ Assume death at age 85 – the insured has recouped all outlay ($102,100) Plus $2,297,900 in dividend income and still delivered $3,848,202 to the beneficiary. It gets better if death occurs later.

POL YR	AGE AT START YR	ANNUAL DIVIDEND	NET PREMIUM	CUM NET PREMIUM	GUARANTEED CASH VALUE	CASH VALUE OF ALL ADDS	NET CASH VALUE	NET DEATH BENEFIT
1	18	$0	$35,000	$35,000	$0	$23,180	$23,180	$1,819,891
2	19	$0	$35,000	$70,000	$8,792	$49,544	$58,336	$1,999,212
3	20	$2,417	$35,000	$105,000	$17,911	$78,466	$96,377	$2,190,611
4	21	$4,110	$35,000	$140,000	$27,357	$110,204	$137,561	$2,388,629
5	22	$5,955	$35,000	$175,000	$37,148	$145,010	$182,158	$2,593,722
6	23	$7,970	$35,000	$210,000	$47,315	$183,196	$230,510	$2,806,440
7	24	$10,167	$35,000	$245,000	$57,842	$225,068	$282,910	$3,027,295
8	25	$12,569	$35,000	$280,000	$68,762	$270,951	$339,713	$3,256,840
9	26	$15,144	-$26,125	$253,875	$80,107	$256,327	$336,434	$3,116,498
10	27	$15,027	$11,375	$265,250	$91,879	$281,720	$373,598	$3,209,403
11	28	$16,745	$11,375	$276,625	$104,059	$309,835	$413,894	$3,309,576
12	29	$18,622	$11,375	$288,000	$116,698	$340,959	$457,658	$3,417,346
13	30	$20,638	-$26,125	$261,875	$129,763	$334,949	$464,713	$3,325,290
14	31	$21,206	$11,375	$273,250	$143,319	$369,920	$513,239	$3,440,364
15	32	$23,617	$11,375	$284,625	$157,350	$408,683	$566,032	$3,564,325
16	33	$26,217	$11,375	$296,000	$171,888	$451,592	$623,480	$3,697,446
17	34	$29,036	-$26,125	$269,875	$186,917	$458,407	$645,325	$3,657,984
18	35	$30,262	$11,375	$281,250	$202,438	$507,324	$709,762	$3,801,810
19	36	$33,401	$11,375	$292,625	$218,466	$561,341	$779,807	$3,955,509
20	37	$36,884	$11,375	$304,000	$234,985	$620,882	$855,867	$4,119,761
21	38	$40,689	-$26,125	$277,875	$251,340	$645,774	$897,115	$4,135,417
22	39	$42,921	$11,375	$289,250	$268,138	$714,356	$982,494	$4,314,533
23	40	$47,226	$11,375	$300,625	$285,361	$789,693	$1,075,054	$4,505,396
24	41	$51,905	$11,375	$312,000	$303,010	$872,256	$1,175,266	$4,708,565
25	42	$56,940	-$26,125	$285,875	$321,101	$922,075	$1,243,176	$4,784,029
26	43	$60,530	$11,375	$297,250	$339,667	$1,017,694	$1,357,361	$5,006,557
27	44	$66,221	$11,375	$308,625	$358,740	$1,122,345	$1,481,084	$5,242,625
28	45	$72,394	$11,375	$320,000	$378,337	$1,236,617	$1,614,954	$5,492,794
29	46	$78,961	-$26,125	$293,875	$398,491	$1,320,818	$1,719,308	$5,633,278
30	47	$84,186	$11,375	$305,250	$419,201	$1,453,702	$1,872,903	$5,907,171
31	48	$91,771	$11,375	$316,625	$440,501	$1,598,484	$2,038,985	$6,196,768
32	49	$99,828	$11,375	$328,000	$462,357	$1,756,014	$2,218,371	$6,502,451
33	50	$108,440	-$26,125	$301,875	$484,819	$1,886,876	$2,371,696	$6,714,743
34	51	$115,918	$11,375	$313,250	$507,871	$2,070,071	$2,577,942	$7,049,584
35	52	$125,996	$11,375	$324,625	$531,528	$2,269,028	$2,800,556	$7,402,958
36	53	$436,756	$11,375	$336,000	$555,775	$2,485,174	$3,040,948	$7,775,805
37	54	$148,578	-$26,125	$309,875	$580,627	$2,679,348	$3,259,975	$8,071,371
38	55	$159,388	$11,375	$321,250	$606,135	$2,930,383	$3,539,515	$8,481,440
39	56	$172,574	$11,375	$332,625	$632,346	$3,202,331	$3,834,677	$8,913,025
40	57	$186,668	$11,375	$344,000	$659,327	$3,496,766	$4,156,092	$9,366,412
41	58	$201,539	-$26,125	$317,875	$687,208	$3,775,037	$4,462,245	$9,755,408
42	59	$215,486	$11,375	$329,250	$715,973	$4,116,394	$4,832,367	$10,250,400
43	60	$232,067	$11,375	$340,625	$745,655	$4,485,354	$5,231,010	$10,769,092
44	61	$250,032	$11,375	$352,000	$776,254	$4,884,048	$5,660,302	$11,313,135
45	62	$269,734	-$26,125	$325,875	$807,656	$5,271,515	$6,082,171	$11,806,657
46	63	$289,850	$11,375	$337,250	$839,794	$5,737,379	$6,577,172	$12,406,125
47	64	$314,833	$11,375	$348,625	$872,619	$6,237,243	$7,109,862	$13,039,948
48	65	$341,691	$0	$348,625	$896,244	$6,767,511	$7,663,755	$13,700,735
49	66	$361,406	-$37,500	$311,125	$920,114	$7,299,461	$8,219,575	$14,321,219
50	67	$390,206	$0	$311,125	$944,279	$7,913,809	$8,858,088	$15,047,961
51	68	$422,643	$0	$311,125	$968,836	$8,575,383	$9,544,219	$15,813,854

POL YR	AGE AT START YR	ANNUAL DIVI-DEND	NET PRE-MIUM	CUM NET PREMIUM	GUARANTEED CASH VALUE	CASH VALUE OF ALL ADDS	NET CASH VALUE	NET DEATH BENEFIT
52	69	$455,760	$0	$311,125	$993,836	$9,288,451	$10,282,287	$16,620,047
53	70	$491,789	-$550,000	-$238,875	$1,019,213	$9,463,038	$10,482,250	$16,533,827
54	71	$501,462	-$550,000	-$788,875	$1,044,834	$9,650,581	$10,695,415	$16,467,876
55	72	$513,479	-$550,000	-$1,338,875	$1,070,522	$9,851,799	$10,922,321	$16,424,650
56	73	$527,479	-$550,000	-$1,888,875	$1,096,062	$10,067,140	$11,163,202	$16,406,151
57	74	$543,422	-$550,000	-$2,438,875	$1,121,291	$40,297,167	$11,418,458	$16,413,867
58	75	$560,963	-$550,000	-$2,988,875	$1,146,127	$10,542,339	$11,688,466	$16,448,187
59	76	$579,276	-$550,000	-$3,538,875	$1,170,521	$10,802,666	$11,973,187	$16,508,382
60	77	$597,652	-$550,000	-$4,088,875	$1,194,506	$11,078,717	$12,273,223	$16,593,347
61	78	$615,967	-$550,000	-$4,638,875	$1,218,163	$11,370,995	$12,589,158	$16,701,549
62	79	$633,756	-$550,000	-$5,188,875	$1,241,460	$11,679,744	$12,921,204	$16,832,158
63	80	$651,799	-$550,000	-$5,738,875	$1,264,381	$12,006,323	$13,270,704	$16,985,703
64	81	$671,095	-$550,000	-$6,288,875	$1,286,778	$12,351,653	$13,638,431	$17,163,807
65	82	$692,399	-$550,000	-$6,838,875	$1,308,470	$12,716,980	$14,025,450	$17,368,956
66	83	$716,373	-$550,000	-$7,388,875	$1,329,312	$13,103,688	$14,432,999	$17,603,664
67	84	$742,912	-$550,000	-$7,938,875	$1,349,220	$13,513,260	$14,862,479	$17,869,907
68	85	$771,564	-$550,000	-$8,488,875	$1,368,178	$13,946,895	$15,315,073	$18,168,676
69	86	$201,481	-$550,000	-$9,038,875	$1,386,269	$14,406,625	$15,792,894	$18,500,711
70	87	$832,589	-$550,000	-$9,588,875	$1,403,558	$14,893,867	$16,297,424	$18,866,289
71	88	$864,430	-$550,000	-$10,138,875	$1,420,241	$15,411,200	$16,831,441	$19,265,467
72	89	$896,840	-$550,000	-$10,688,875	$1,436,482	$15,961,130	$17,397,612	$19,698,436
73	90	$929,988	-$550,000	-$11,238,875	$1,452,510	$16,546,945	$17,999,454	$20,165,386
74	91	$963,859	-$550,000	-$11,788,875	$1,468,603	$17,172,805	$18,641,608	$20,666,623
75	92	$998,618	-$550,000	-$12,338,875	$1,485,122	$17,843,816	$19,328,938	$21,202,153

FEMALE, AGE 18, $717,218 Life Paid-up at Age 65

PREFERRED	$11,375
Paid-Up Additions Rider	$23,625
Total Premium	$35,000

1. $35,000 represents premiums going to life insurance policy instead of going to the cost of getting a degree.

2. -$26,125 represents an automobile purchase of $37,500 less a payment of $11,375 to premium instead of to a finance company or bank.

3. $11,375 represents a premium payment instead of a car payment to a bank.

4. $10,282,287 is the illustrated cash value at age 70.

5. -$550,000 represents annual income from dividends at retirement time.

6. Assume death at age 85—the insured has recouped all outlay ($311,125) plus $8,488,875 in dividend income and still delivered $18,168,676 to the beneficiary. It gets better if death occurs later.

WHAT IF I AM UNINSURABLE?

 AND others have asked, "What if I am uninsurable? After all, not everyone is blessed with perfect health." For those people, consider this possibility: Father is 50 years old and is uninsurable — or highly "rated" — on account of occupation or poor health. He wants to adopt the *Infinite Banking Concept* to provide "passive income" at his age 70 for the balance of his life. Please notice that I did not say "retirement" income — I'm dropping that word from my vocabulary. Passive income is money that comes in every year and you don't have to do anything to receive it. In fact, you can't do anything about it — it just appears!

Mother agrees that this is a worthy goal. She is about the same age as her husband and they have a 23 year old daughter, Jill, who is in excellent health.

To accomplish their goal they decide to put $20,000 per year into a policy on Jill. $10,000 will go into the base policy (Life Paid-Up at age 64) and $10,000 into a Paid-Up Additions Rider.

They do this for twenty years and Father is now age 70. At this point they decide to cease premium payments and to start drawing "passive income" in the amount of $28,500 per year. This is done by surrendering cash values of Paid-Up Additions. This income is tax-free until the amount withdrawn equals the cost basis of the policy (the premiums paid out).

Fifteen years later Father is 85 years old and has drawn out cash values of dividend additions equal to the premiums paid into the policy. He has no cost basis at all. If he is still living at this point, and wants to continue receiving tax-free income, he could simply switch to policy loans which are income tax-free.

Assume that he dies at age 85. Note that the cash value of the policy is $1,110,726. This sounds like life insurance on Father, doesn't it? Father paid premiums for 20 years — then withdrew every dollar paid out — on a tax-free basis — and delivered $1,110,726 to his daughter at her age 57.

In this illustration, the assumption is that Jill simply let the insurance company manage the policy for the remainder of her life. Therefore, no additional premiums — and at her age 70 she decides to surrender cash values of dividend additions in the amount of $150,000 for the balance of her life.

Assume her death at age 90 — and she has withdrawn "passive income" totaling $3,150,000 — and she still delivered a $2,378,391 death benefit to the next generation.

All during the period of premium payments and withdrawals Jill *could have* been using the cash values to finance automobiles, homes, and anything that your imagination allows. If she follows the principles taught earlier in this book, then the results would be *much greater* than depicted in this illustration.

POLICY YEAR	AGE AT START YR	ANNUAL DIV	NET PREM	CUM NET PREM	GUAR CASH VAL	CV OF ALL ADDS	NET CASH VAL	NET DEATH BENEFIT
1	23	$0	$20,000	$20,000	$0	$9,816	$9,816	$1,328,111
2	24	$0	$20,000	$40,000	$8,559	$20,640	$29,198	$1,392,428
3	25	$679	$20,000	$60,000	$17,458	$32,174	$49,633	$1,458,760
4	26	$1,024	$20,000	$80,000	$26,686	$44,696	$71,382	$1,525,369
5	27	$1,621	$20,000	$100,000	$36,255	$58,351	$94,606	$1,593,560
6	28	$2,357	$20,000	$120,000	$46,177	$73,238	$119,415	$1,663,758
7	29	$3,100	$20,000	$140,000	$56,452	$89,465	$145,917	$1,736,140
8	30	$3,926	$20,000	$160,000	$67,107	$107,113	$174,220	$1,810,759
9	31	$4,794	$20,000	$180,000	$78,127	$126,289	$204,416	$1,887,633
10	32	$5,724	$20,000	$200,000	$89,564	$147,094	$236,658	$1,966,838
11	33	$6,669	$20,000	$220,000	$101,405	$169,645	$271,050	$2,048,387
12	34	$7,737	$20,000	$240,000	$113,637	$194,130	$307,767	$2,132,407
13	35	$8,906	$20,000	$260,000	$126,286	$220,914	$347,200	$2,219,465
14	36	$10,392	$20,000	$280,000	$139,351	$250,225	$389,576	$2,310,556
15	37	$12,029	$20,000	$300,000	$152,808	$282,229	$435,037	$2,405,963
16	38	$13,782	$20,000	$320,000	$166,668	$317,138	$483,806	$2,505,840
17	39	$15,672	$20,000	$340,000	$180,908	$355,151	$536,059	$2,610,402
18	40	$17,711	$20,000	$360,000	$195,538	$396,521	$592,060	$2,719,877
19	41	$19,909	$20,000	$380,000	$210,535	$441,432	$651,968	$2,834,466
20	42	$22,237	$20,000	$400,000	$225,923	$490,421	$716,045	$2,954,289
21	43	$24,718	-$28,500	$371,500	$241,122	$491,712	$732,834	$2,905,890
22	44	$25,692	-$28,500	$343,000	$256,750	$494,268	$751,018	$2,862,424
23	45	$26,691	-$28,500	$314,500	$272,820	$497,816	$770,635	$2,823,705
24	46	$27,708	-$28,500	$286,000	$289,344	$502,469	$791,813	$2,789,573
25	47	$28,784	-$28,500	$257,500	$306,348	$508,322	$814,670	$2,759,964
26	48	$29,911	-$28,500	$229,000	$323,844	$515,456	$839,300	$2,734,807
27	49	$31,105	-$28,500	$200,500	$341,820	$523,960	$865,779	$2,714,053
28	50	$32,356	-$28,500	$172,000	$360,288	$533,955	$894,283	$2,697,677
29	51	$33,720	-$28,500	$143,500	$379,274	$545,667	$924,941	$2,685,718
30	52	$35,152	-$28,500	$115,000	$398,777	$559,034	$957,811	$2,678,090
31	53	$36,628	-$28,500	$86,500	$418,786	$574,027	$992,812	$2,674,511
32	54	$37,992	-$28,500	$58,000	$439,324	$590,706	$1,030,030	$2,674,580
33	55	$39,363	-$28,500	$29,500	$460,418	$609,200	$1,069,618	$2,678,191
34	56	$40,824	-$29,500	$0	$482,118	$628,608	$1,110,726	$2,682,897
35	57	$42,328	$0	$0	$504,487	$681,397	$1,185,884	$2,761,411
36	58	$44,844	$0	$0	$527,613	$738,262	$1,265,875	$2,843,568
37	59	$47,400	$0	$0	$551,509	$799,497	$1,351,006	$2,929,355
38	60	$50,152	$0	$0	$576,214	$865,321	$1,441,535	$3,018,852
39	61	$53,015	$0	$0	$601,688	$936,205	$1,537,893	$3,112,336

FEMALE, AGE 23, PREFERRED PLUS, Life Paid-Up at Age 64

Premium	$10,000
Paid-Up Additions Rider	$10,000
Total Premium	$20,000

POLICY YEAR	AGE AT START YR	ANNUAL DIV	NET PREM	CUM NET PREM	GUAR CASH VAL	CV OF ALL ADDS	NET CASH VAL	NET DEATH BENEFIT
40	62	$56,293	$0	$0	$627,907	$1,012,572	$1,640,479	$3,210,381
41	63	$59,971	$0	$0	$654,783	$1,094,882	$1,749,664	$3,313,626
42	64	$64,173	$0	$0	$672,834	$1,185,578	$1,858,412	$3,433,683
43	65	$60,511	$0	$0	$691,050	$1,282,792	$1,973,842	$3,551,818
44	66	$65,117	$0	$0	$709,455	$1,387,095	$2,096,550	$3,675,789
45	67	$70,138	$0	$0	$728,087	$1,498,835	$2,226,922	$3,805,760
46	68	$75,311	$0	$0	$747,023	$1,618,253	$2,365,276	$3,941,461
47	69	$80,439	$0	$0	$766,299	$1,745,978	$2,512,277	$4,082,920
48	70	$85,968	-$150,000	-$150,000	$785,865	$1,722,692	$2,508,557	$3,977,431
49	71	$85,963	-$150,000	-$300,000	$805,621	$1,698,610	$2,504,231	$3,874,986
50	72	$86,382	-$150,000	-$450,000	$825,427	$1,673,594	$2,499,021	$3,775,830
51	73	$86,911	-$150,000	-$600,000	$845,120	$1,647,843	$2,492,963	$3,680,334
52	74	$87,900	-$150,000	-$750,000	$864,573	$1,621,267	$2,485,840	$3,588,623
53	75	$88,947	-$150,000	-$900,000	$883,723	$1,993,867	$2,477,590	$3,500,545
54	76	$90,012	-$150,000	-$1,050,000	$902,532	$1,565,494	$2,468,026	$3,415,739
55	77	$90,895	-$150,000	-$1,200,000	$921,025	$1,535,743	$2,456,769	$3,333,420
56	78	$91,245	-$150,000	-$1,350,000	$939,266	$1,504,676	$2,443,942	$3,253,134
57	79	$91,488	-$150,000	-$1,500,000	$957,230	$1,472,146	$2,429,376	$3,174,569
58	80	$91,562	-$150,000	-$1,650,000	$974,903	$1,438,146	$2,413,049	$3,097,532
59	81	$91,590	-$150,000	-$1,800,000	$992,172	$1,402,649	$2,394,820	$3,021,995
60	82	$91,685	-$150,000	-$1,950,000	$1,008,898	$1,365,634	$2,374,632	$2,947,982
61	83	$91,868	-$150,000	-$2,100,000	$1,024,968	$1,326,849	$2,351,817	$2,875,231
62	84	$91,853	-$150,000	-$2,250,000	$1,040,318	$1,286,547	$2,326,865	$2,803,837
63	85	$92,073	-$150,000	-$2,400,000	$1,054,936	$1,244,584	$2,299,519	$2,733,540
64	86	$92,066	-$150,000	-$2,550,000	$1,068,885	$1,200,554	$2,269,439	$2,663,646
65	87	$91,497	-$150,000	-$2,700,000	$1,082,215	$1,154,235	$2,236,451	$2,593,637
66	88	$90,579	-$150,000	-$2,850,000	$1,095,079	$1,105,487	$2,200,565	$2,523,061
67	89	$89,315	-$150,000	-$3,000,000	$1,107,601	$1,054,075	$2,161,676	$2,451,452
68	90	$87,661	-$150,000	-$3,150,000	$1,119,960	$999,810	$2,119,770	$2,378,391

POINTS TO CONSIDER

1. There are only two sources of income — people at work and money at work. In the typical American family, through the first half of the Twentieth Century, the father worked outside the home and the mother managed the home, nurturing the family and instilling spiritual values as the children matured. Now it is widely accepted that "a family can't make it without both spouses working outside the home. It takes two incomes 'just to make ends meet.'" Could it be a fact that this modern family has no money at work?

2. If you knew, at passive income time, that you would be getting back everything that you paid into a system — tax free — would you object to putting more money in it?

3. When you get paid for your work, you put *all* of it into "someone else's bank" and then write checks from the account to buy the things of life. So, "someone else's bank" gets *all of your money*. If you owned a banking system, wouldn't you want to run *all* of your business through your bank? If this is so, then life insurance premiums paid each year should ultimately equal annual income. This can't be done immediately. It will take the average person about twenty years to reach this level. If this message is taught to succeeding generations, then a perpetual banking system can be achieved.

4. When government creates a problem (onerous taxation) and then turns around and grants you an exception to the problem they created (any tax-qualified plan) aren't you just a little bit suspicious that you are being manipulated? Tax-qualified retirement plans were all created under the guise of "giving you a break." First, there were pension plans for corporate employees, and then came HR-10 plans for partners and sole proprietors, and finally, IRA's for individuals. Now everyone "had an exception" to the IRS Code. If the government really wanted to "give you a break" — all they had to do is *cut out the taxes!* Do you really think they want to do that?

5. Wealth has got to reside somewhere. Where would you prefer to have it reside?

- Real Estate? Then take a look around and see what happens when one needs liquidity. Real estate is very much a "frozen asset."

- The Stock Market? Then, try reading from my *Recommended Reading for Those Interested in the Stock Market* on page 91 in this book. Until you have done so, are you qualified to make an intelligent decision about such action?

- Or, free contract with other free persons (Life Insurance)? From this base of financial operation you can do any of the other things in life that you desire.

6. You finance everything you buy. You either pay interest to someone else or you give up interest you could have earned elsewhere. There are no exceptions.

7. Your need for finance, during your lifetime, exceeds your need for life insurance protection. If you solve for your need for finance through life insurance cash values, you will end up with so much life insurance; you can't get it past the underwriters. You will have to insure every person in which you have an insurable interest.

EPILOGUE

Any illustration contained in this book does not represent the performance of any particular life insurance company and in no way implies guarantees of any kind. These illustrations are simply teaching tools to show how life insurance can be used to achieve certain goals.

The Infinite Banking Concept is a teaching organization and is not affiliated with any life insurance organization and in no way implies that a person will be guaranteed results comparable to anything shown in this book, no more than a school or professor at a school can guarantee a person financial success from taking a certain course of study or procedure. In fact, if a person obeys the principles outlined in the book the performance can exceed the results that are depicted in these illustrations.

GLOSSARY OF TERMS

Banking* - The business of a bank, originally restricted to money changing and now devoted to taking money on deposit subject to check or draft, loaning money and credit and **any other associated form of general dealing in money or credit.**

Capital* - Accumulated possessions calculated to bring in income: accumulated assets, resources, sources of strength, or advantages utilized to aid in accomplishing an end or furthering a pursuit.

Capitalization Period - The time required to actually create a pool of money with which to start your own banking system. *It definitely is not something that you can do overnight!* You might have all the necessary capital (money), but there is still the element *of time.* It is like the process of getting a college degree - you may have the necessary funds on hand to pay for the degree, but you *still must go through the required curriculum.* Building your personal banking system through the medium of dividend- paying whole life insurance will take as little as one and one-half years, but you still need to continue the *capitalization phase* for as much as ten *or more* years - the longer the period, the more strength of your system.

Cash Value - The cash value on any policy anniversary to which premiums have been paid is: the then present value of future benefits provided by the policy; less: the then present value factors for each year remaining in the premium payment period. The cash value at any time during a policy year is the value on the date to which premiums have been paid, adjusted to the date of surrender.

Characters in the Play - All the necessary functions in a given business, e.g., Stockholder, Bondholder, CD holder, Administrator, Borrower, etc. This is in the context of my statement, "on the of finance most people don't understand what the play is about - but worse than that, they get the *characters* mixed up!

Co-Generation - A term used in the production of electrical power acknowledging the fact that there are *many sources* of the generation of power within the distribution system, many of whom are both *producers and consumers* of power.

Classification* - The act of grouping into classes that have systematic relations usually founded on common properties. (You classify things on the basis of their *major characteristics.* A life insurance policy with a mutual, dividend-paying company is a *gross misclassification* of a financial instrument. It has much more in common with the concept of banking.)

Contingency Fund - The amount that an insurance company retains as surplus after paying death claims, expenses and dividends to policyholders. This is a significant measure of the strength of a particular company and an indication of its ability to pay dividends in the future

Dividends - The earnings of a life insurance policy, based on the company's mortality, expense, and investment experience during the year. When dividends are used to buy additional paid-up insurance at *no cost to the owner* the cash value of the additions becomes guaranteed at that time. This value *will increase* with time but *cannot decrease.*

Entity - Something that has independent or separate existence.

Finance* - (noun) The system that includes the circulation of money, the granting of credit, the making of investments, and the provision of banking facilities.(verb) To provide with necessary funds in order to achieve a desired end. *(You finance everything you buy - you either pay interest to others, or you give up interest that you could have earned elsewhere).*

Gate-keeper or Toll-taker - Any intermediary

that controls access to a pool of money (bank) e.g. GMAC, Associates Finance, GE Credit, etc.

Gopher - Any administrator within a banking system. Bankers don't work at the Bank - *gophers* work at the Bank and they are given long titles to offset their low pay scale. Real Bankers are found on the golf course, or in all probability running some other business.

Great Wall of China - The barrier limiting access to the pool of money except through the gate-keeper.

Interest* - The price paid for borrowing money generally expressed as a percentage of the amount borrowed paid in one year.

Lease* - A contract by which one conveys property for a term of years, or at will for a specified rent or compensation.

Lessee* - One taking possession of property under a lease.

Lessor* - One that surrenders possession of property under a lease.

Mortgage* - A conveyance of property upon condition that operates as a lien securing the payment of the money or performance of an obligation so that the mortgagee may under certain conditions take possession and may foreclose according to the stipulated terms.

Owner* - One that has the legal or rightful title whether the possessor or not.

Philosophy* - A search for the underlying causes and principles of reality: a quest for truth through logical reasoning rather than factual observation: a critical examination of the grounds for fundamental beliefs and an analysis of the basic concepts employed in the expression of such beliefs.

Process* - The action of continuously going along through each of a succession of acts, events, or development stages: the action of being progressively advanced or progressively done.

Stock* - Capital for investment or direct use in business: principal as distinguished from interest. (If you want to have a little fun, look this one up in an unabridged dictionary!)

Senior Executive Vice-President - A gopher at a bank or life insurance company.

Steal* - To practice theft: take the property of another. (For our purposes we are speaking of making policy loans *without setting up—and **completing** a repayment schedule.)*

System* - A complex unity formed of many often diverse parts subject to a common plan or serving a common purpose. (This dictionary continued the definition for 9 inches of column of very small print!)

Trust* - A property interest held by one person or other entity, for the benefit of another.

*The foregoing definitions were taken from Webster's Third New International Dictionary

BOOK RECOMMENDATIONS

 *Get the following from Foundation for Economic Education, Inc., 30 South Broadway, Irvington on Hudson, NY 10533. www.fee.org*

The Law by Frederic Bastiat. A great "giveaway" book. Buy them in quantity from FEE

The Mainspring of Human Progress by Henry Grady Weaver (Another good giveaway)

Get the following from Ludwig von Mises Institute, 518 West Magnolia Ave., Auburn, AL 36832-4528. www.mises.org

A Century of War by John Denson

A History of Money & Banking in the United States by Murray Rothbard

Age of Inflation by Hans F. Sennholz

Democracy, The God that Failed by Hans-Hermann Hoppe

Economics for Real People by Gene Callahan

Economics in One Lesson by Henry Hazlitt

For Good and For Evil" the Impact of Taxes on the Course of Civilization* by Charles Adams "Behind every significant event in history there is a tax story."

How Capitalism Saved America by Thomas DiLorenzo. The untold history of our country from the Pilgrims to the present.

Human Action by Ludwig von Mises

Lincoln Unmasked by Thomas DiLorenzo

Speaking of Liberty by Llewellyn H. Rockwell, Jr.

The Case Against The Fed by Murray Rothbard

The Myth of National Defense by Hans-Hermann Hoppe

The Politically Incorrect Guide to American History by Tom Woods

The Quotable Mises by Mark Thornton

The Real Lincoln by Thomas DiLorenzo

The Road to Serfdom by F. A. Hayek

What Has The Government Done To Our Money by Murray Rothbard

Get the following from Laissez Faire Books, 938 Howard Street, #202, San Francisco, CA 94103. www.lfb.com

Atlas Shrugged by Ayn Rand

Discovery of Freedom: Man's Struggle Against Authority by Rose Wilder Lane

FDR's Folly by Jim Powell. This one helps you to better understand the mess our country is in today.

Going Broke by Degree by Richard Vedder

Just Get Out of the Way: How Government Can Help Business in Poor Countries by Robert E. Anderson

The End of Money and the Struggle for Financial Privacy by Richard W. Rahn

The Incredible Bread Machine by R. W. Grant

The Mystery of Capital by Hernando de Soto

The Transfer Society by David N. Laband and George C. McClintock

Wilson's War by Jim Powell

Get the following from CASHFLOW Technologies, Inc., 6611 N. 64th Place, Paradise Valley, AZ 85253 www.cashflowtech.com

Rich Dad, Poor Dad by Robert Kiyosaki

The Cashflow Quadrant by Robert Kiyosaki

Rich Dad's Phrophecy by Robert Kiyosaki*ust Get Out of the Way* by Robert E. Anderson

---

The following books are generally available from most on-line book sellers.

Against The Gods The Remarkable Story of Risk by Peter L. Bernstein.

At the Crest of the Tidal Wave - A forecast of the great Bear Market by Robert R. Prechter, Jr. You might read this one before the one listed above. Get them from www.elliotwave.com

Chance in Life and in the Markets by Nassim Nicholas Taleb

EVA the Real Key Creating Wealth by Al Ehrbar

Fooled by Randomness: The Hidden Role Chance in Life and in the Markets by Hassim Nicholas Taleb

Foundations of Economic Value Added by James L. Grant

How to Think Like Einstein by Scott Thorpe

Inside American Education by Tom Sowell; this one will go a long way towards explaining the root of most of our problems in America.

Parliament of Whores by P. J. O'Rouke

Social Security: False Consciousness and Crisis by John Attarian

Spiritual Economics: The Principles and Process of True Prosperity by Eric Butterworth

Stealing America - A History of Corruption From Jamestown to Reagan by Nathan Miller

The Demise of the Dollar... and Why It's Great For Your Investments by Addison Wiggin

The Discovery of Freedom by Rose Wilder Lane

The FairTax Book by Neal Boortz and John Linder

The God of the Machine by Isabel Patterson

The March of Folly by Barbara Tuchman

The Millionaire Next Door by Thomas Stanley and William Danko

RECOMMENDED READING FOR THOSE INTERESTED IN THE STOCK MARKET

The Pension Idea by Paul Poirot. Get them from our website: www.infinitebanking.org

The Prayer of Jabez by Bruce Wilkinson

The Proud Tower by Barbara Tuchman

The Purpose Driven Life by Rick Warren

The Retirement Myth by Craig S. Karpel

The Richest Man in Babylon by George Clason

The Social Security Fraud by Abraham Ellis

The Sovereign Individual by James Davidson and Lord Rees-Mogg

Understanding the Modern Culture Wars - The Essentials of Western Civilization by Paul A. Cleveland, Boundary Stone, www.boundarystone.net, phone 205-305-5862

When in the Course of Human Events by Charles Adams

Who Moved My Cheese? by Spencer Johnson, M.D and Kenneth H. Blanchard

Conquer the Crash - You can Survive and Prosper in a Deflationary Depression by Robert R. Prechter, Jr. This book is essential reading.

Den of Thieves by James Stewart

Devil Take the Hindmost: A History of Financial Speculation by Edward Chancellor

Eat The Rich by P. J. O'Rourke

Economic Value Added by Al Ehrbar

Empire of Debt : The Rise of an Epic Financial Crisis by William Bonner and Addison Wiggin

Extraordinary Popular Delusions and the Madness of Crowds by Andrew Tobias and Charles Mackay

F.I.A.S.C.O. by Frank Partnoy

Financial Reckoning Day - Surviving the Soft Depression of the 21st Century by William Bonner

Inventing Money by Nicholas Dunbar

Money and Wealth in the New Millennium by Norm Franz

Myths, Lies and Downright Stupidity by John Stossel

The Battle for the Soul of Capitalism by John C. Bogle

The Creature from Jekyll Island by G. Edward Griffin *"It's not Federal. There is no reserve. And it is not a bank!"* Get this book from American Media, P. O. Box 4646, Westlake Village, CA 91359-1646. Or call 800-595-6596. Ask for quantity discounts. Or, try www.realtyzone.com

The Pirates of Manhattan by Barry Dyke. Get it from our website: www.infinitebanking.org or Barry's site - www.thepiratesofmanhattan.com

The Trouble with Mutual Funds by Richard Rutner Financial Press, Inc. 888-959-3565 www.troublewithmutualfunds.com

What Goes Up: The Uncensored History of Modern Wall Street as Told by the Bankers, Brokers, CEOs, and Scoundrels Who Made It Happen by Eric Weiner

BIOGRAPHICAL INFORMATION

The Infinite Banking Concept was conceived by R. Nelson Nash in the early 1980's as a result of his personal experience in several business activities.

• He received his BS degree in Forestry from the University of Georgia in 1952 and worked as a forestry consultant for 10 years in North Carolina.

• He spent over 30 years as an agent for two major mutual life insurance companies.

• He has been active in real estate investments for over 45 years.

• He has spent over 40 years in the study of Economics (The Austrian School).

• He formed a "think tank" of people who have become advocates of The Infinite Banking Concept. At present there are more than 250 members and they are from all over the United States.